# Walking

## on Eggshells

# Walking

## on Eggshells

When Dogs Behave
Aggressively on the Lead

Nadin Matthews

CADMOS

# Imprint

Copyright © 2012 Cadmos Publishing Limited, Richmond, UK
Copyright of original edition © 2011 Cadmos Verlag GmbH,
Schwarzenbek, Germany

Layout and design: Ravenstein + Partner, Verden
Setting: Das Agenturhaus, Munich
Cover drawing: Robertino Nikolic
Inside photography: Robertino Nikolic and others
Translation: Helen Mc Kinnon
Editorial of the original edition: Johanna Esser
Editorial of this edition: Christopher Long
Printed by: Westermann Druck, Zwickau

Printed in Germany

ISBN: 978-0-85788-205-9

# Foreword

For Leo and Levi

In memory of
Jeanny and Vivi

# Foreword

So here I sit, it's 9.45 am and I've actually finished my book. All that's missing is the foreword, which I have already started several times. Sometimes it's funny, sometimes it's serious, then it's madly technical and then back to funny again, but I've never managed to get any further. I wrote the book in one go, I've even chosen the images and now this. I have arranged to go for a walk with friends at 2 pm. They've got a new dog and I don't want to have to let them down; after all, I'm curious.

Before we became friends they were both my clients and came to me with their one-year-old Podengo Portugueso Medio (medium Portuguese hound) for training advice. They had taken on the young male dog, Bolt, straight from a Portuguese animal shelter, more or less as a "surprise package" and that is exactly what he was.

Bolt was described as a good-natured dog, but, unfortunately, that wasn't really the case. When he was on his lead, you could rely on him to snap whenever another dog approached and, now and then, his owner's thigh would also bear the brunt of his redirected aggression. If he could reach the other dog, he would bite it immediately and the few attempts at letting him run free also ended badly for the other dog in a similar way. He had no idea how else to behave around other members of his species.

The consultation, which took place at intervals, lasted for a period of one year – a fairly long time. There were improvements and there were setbacks; but in the end, Bolt was able to change stably with the help of his owners. He now walks past other dogs quietly and can also communicate appropriately off the lead. This was actually a good time to finally enjoy walks together.

Yet the better things went with Bolt, the more his owners wanted another dog. This often happens with people. When we spoke about it yet again, I recommended an older, quiet and confident female that could guide Bolt and pose few difficulties herself. I offered to help them choose and even suggested one or two dogs that I could introduce them to, but nothing came of it.

On our last walk together, we had already been wandering in the forest for two hours when the following sentence quite casually cropped up: "We probably won't make it to the Easter bonfire on Saturday, because we're in Portugal that day." As I looked questioningly at them both, they added almost sheepishly, "We're going to look at a dog. She's called Tita, she's a six-month-old, medium Portuguese hound who's in the dogs' home there and she looks just like Bolt." I had to smile and almost laughed. That is exactly why I like people so much.

I don't know whether they both expected me to give them a professional talk on the topic of "sensibly choosing a second dog", but it was clear – of course they would fly to Portugal; of course they would bring the dog home with them; of course they would have an infinitely hard time with her; of course they would curse their decision every now and then; of course they would love the little dog and have many happy moments together.

People don't choose dogs based on common sense, but because they associate certain qualities with them. If we were all sensible then we wouldn't have dogs at all and we probably wouldn't have any children either and that would be a shame. Why should I be able to judge what's right and what's wrong? Because I'm a dog trainer? Then I'd have misunderstood my role. Life is too colourful to be calculated and I can easily understand the very decisions that are difficult to comprehend.

So, as a friend, I will be happy for both of them. And, as an advisor, I will support them as they train their dog. That's my job and I love it.

And that is why I can only be thankful for the people, their dogs and the uniqueness that represent my work and that, at the same time, have also written my foreword.

Nadin Matthews

# The problem
## and the explanation

The intensity with which Bolt expressed his aggression on the lead is certainly an exception. The problem itself, on the other hand, isn't. Along with hunting problems, aggressive behaviour on the lead is one of the most common reasons why people seek one-to-one advice. Lead aggression does not boil down to unwanted barking. It is about so much more, both for dogs and for people.

## A typical sequence of events or just a normal evening?

The anxiety begins with the weather forecast and she can feel it starting to grip her every evening, as the closing credits of the news roll – fear of 800 metres; fear of the evening walk. Who could still be out with their dog at this time? This question preoccupies her three times a day. When did this fear of going for a walk actually begin? Before she can come up with the answer, a name pops into her head: Asco. If everything goes according to plan, he should be back at home again now. She really doesn't know much about Asco's owner, other than when he goes out with his uncastrated male dog. There was a time when she thought about inviting him round for coffee so she could get to know him better, but that was when Ben was little and fear did not join them on their walks together.

Now this anxiety dictates that she should do the exact opposite; namely, avoid every encounter. She stands in the hallway and reaches for the lead. Ben jumps out of his basket as if he had been waiting for this sound and tears past her, straight to the front door. He is ready for his big appearance. For one last time today, he wants to show the world that he is the king of the street.

She doesn't feel very king-like at all and looks at him anxiously. The behaviour Ben displays is what experts would call appetitive behaviour, but you could also say that he starts looking for other dogs as soon as his owner reaches for the lead and that his expectations for the walk are high. If he were a person, he would put on his leather jacket and run his hand through his hair, full of anticipation, before grinning and trying out a pose in front of the mirror. However, she is not a dog expert. His actions represent her problem and she knows that if he is behaving like this now, he will be difficult outside. She reaches for the canine headcollar almost as a reflex action. Well, you never know what, or rather who, you might meet.

For good measure, she takes his favourite ball with her, along with a bag of chopped-up sausage. Maybe this time she will be able to use them to distract him.

Armed with this arsenal of "magic bullets", also known as "aids" in dog training, she moves on to the next steps. Like an old rehearsed ballad, she asks Ben to sit. As always, he only reacts after the third warning and, as always, he seems annoyed as he does so. Yet she remains resolute and only puts on his lead when he has sat down. It feels good when, at least in this situation, he responds to her.

There is something wrong with this picture. Shouldn't she be able to relax and happily enjoy the lovely evening air with her dog? After all, she got a dog to get outside more – a loyal companion for her morning jog and the antidote to her office job. She wanted a healthy, sporty dog that would challenge her and decided on a German Shepherd cross. He is agile, but she can no longer go on her old jogging route with him, because there are too many other dogs there. She has thought of everything. He has the best food, chew bones to clean his teeth, dog-appropriate toys, the best veterinary care and she takes him to dog training classes regularly. But despite all of this, she can't even go for a walk when, where and how she likes.

It is the same for many people. Every day, people venture out onto the street with their dog on the lead and a bad feeling in their stomach. Even the minutes before going for a walk are full of tension. This does not go unnoticed by the dog. In his laws of communication, Paul Watzlawick formulated that "communication is always circular". That means that the reaction of one communication partner is, at the same time, an action that the other reacts to in turn. Or in translation, Ben tallies up the time with his owner's mood and knows that it is time to go out and that every meeting with another dog will be a highlight. By moving quickly and excitedly between his owner and the door, he tries to hurry along the start of the walk and it works every time – from his point of view at least.

That his owner has pocketed the ball and the food has also not escaped his notice. They give her security and him two more reasons to rush through the door with stiff legs and his tail in the air. After all, he has a lot to do and to defend. Loosely according to the maxim, "my owner, my food, my prey", the walk can begin for him. He starts his evening walk with his chest proudly swelled

*Owner and dog have the enemy in their sights. Shortening the lead is a safety precaution for the owner, but equally a meaningful signal for the dog.*

*The owner unwillingly gets involved in the conflict and becomes an important part of everything that happens.*

while she looks tense. He is going to show his own strength, while she is going to war.

As she frantically scours the street for any potential dogs and owners, Ben makes his olfactory contribution by urinating on other dogs' markings. For him, this is a great division of labour. She works visually and her body language will immediately signal to him whether another dog is coming, while he focuses on the olfactory search. Every tree, every lamp post and every corner give Ben information about the current situation in his street. They have all been here. Sam, Fee and Quentin. And Henry. That pesky sausage dog should think himself lucky that he got castrated a few months ago. And Lola! She's been on heat for a week. Admittedly, Ben hasn't seen her again since, but he can smell her every day. His testosterone levels tell him that he would be the right man for her and there can only be one.

Suddenly, he turns a corner. Asco! "What's he doing out at this time?" she asks herself in desperation and within seconds has checked for possible escape routes. It's hopeless. There's no way she can take a different route and still make it look like a coincidence and if she turns round now she will lose face in front of Asco's owner.

She tries to get herself under control but her pulse is beginning to race. She shortens the lead and embarks upon the anticipated conflict with a sharp "heel". Ben knows the ropes. "Short lead" means there's another dog coming. When combined with the command "heel", it means the other dog is in my fighting class. She had hoped that Ben would come to her side, but he immediately starts pulling on the lead.

He is in peak form. Intently and with a steady gaze, he marches straight up to Asco. As she glances back and forth be-

*The conflict escalates as the dogs draw level. Thoughts about training go out of the window as the owner focuses on holding onto the dog.*

tween Ben and Asco, her breathing and pulse rate increase further and her palms begin to sweat. As you might expect from a "real man", Ben plays the hero and signals to his owner, "I'll take care of this."

Like an echo, she can still hear the voice of her trainer in her ear: "Relax, otherwise you'll reinforce his behaviour." But how is she supposed to relax now? And where's this dog trainer when you need her anyway? She knows she shouldn't do it, but she can't stand it any longer: "It's okay, Ben. It's only Asco." Of course, she didn't need to tell Ben this, because he already knew, but he will notice that his owner ascribes the same importance to the whole situation as he does.

"You have to be more important than the other dog. Get his attention on you." The words are hammering in her head. She fiddles about in her pocket nervously. It's now too late for the canine headcollar, so she tries to bring the ball into play. "Look Ben, your ball!" He seems troubled. How can she wave our prey around when there's another male dog coming? He tries to concentrate in spite of the ball and starts to fix his gaze on Asco. She knows what that means. With the tunnel vision of a ski jumper, he lunges powerfully at the end of the lead.

Just in time, she manages to hold onto the leather lead with both hands. Ben is in his element. His owner is worried about staying on her feet and stares as if paralysed at her dog, whose barking sounds unnaturally loud in the still evening. She tries to counter with a "sit", follows up with a "down" and then a loud "no", but he seems to have understood "attack". It is all in vain. Ben stands on his hind legs, almost hanging himself,

as he rages at the other dog with his lip curled, probably feeling happy that his owner shares his hobby. It's just so much nicer to provoke and antagonise in pairs.

Asco's owner smiles and says something that sounds like "good evening". What was meant as a pleasant social gesture sounds to her like an expression of his superiority and pity for her. How could she have ever liked him? He doesn't have a problem holding his dog. Asco isn't pulling, while Ben, on the other hand, is. He has managed to pull her over the pavement more than once. This time he doesn't manage, but she is ready nevertheless. Once Asco and his owner have passed, Ben, now back on all fours again, pants noisily after them one more time, shakes himself and gives a little jump, jostling his owner. He feels triumphant; she feels miserable. They both know that there's always next time.

300 more metres of evening walk. The lights are going out in many of the windows. Ben lifts his leg several more times and, slowly, she begins to relax. One last corner. They've made it, no one else is around. Next time, she says to herself, I'll go after the night-time news. Nobody will be around then. The TV is still on at home. The whodunnit has started. Her drama is over.

## Why does he do it?

Why is my dog aggressive when he is on his lead? This question is as popular among dog owners as it is difficult to answer, and it assumes that there is one reason or cause for the behaviour. However, if we look at the complexity of social communication, the question becomes almost impossible to answer. The answer could be because he never gets to walk off his lead, so he is frustrated; because he is defending his owner or his territory; because he is fundamentally under-exercised and only gets ten minutes outdoors; because he is currently going through puberty and his hormones are confusing him; because his owner is frightened of other dogs and doesn't act confidently as a result; because he is defending any food or toys that have been brought along; because he broke a leg as a young dog and did not have any contact with other canines as a result or is in pain at the moment; because his owners unwittingly praise him for it or because he has greater potential for aggression towards other dogs because of his breed. Yes, all of those reasons are correct or could be correct. There may be many factors, but rarely ever just one reason.

But it isn't just that. Like a stone that falls into the water and makes ripples, factors have effects within a system. They cause reactions that, in turn, constitute actions that are reacted to. As if in a spiral, the behaviour of one determines the behaviour of the other. In the end, it becomes clear that there is no tangible beginning and that the result is greater than the sum of its parts. Communication amplifies everything, in that there may originally have been a clear motive for the dog to act aggressively, but a real problem develops as a result of the human reaction and judgement of the behaviour. The owner becomes an important part of the aggressive behaviour and, as a result, keeps the problem going, even if the dog's original motive no longer exists. As the description of Ben and his owner shows, misunderstandings be-

*Just looking at the canine symptom carrier is not enough to explain the problem.*

tween dog and owner, along with the dog's various motives, are mainly responsible for the problem increasing in intensity.

This is because dogs do not live in a vacuum; they are part of a social group within which they interact. They establish individual relationships and roles on which they depend and through which they develop their self-image. Dogs are born with different

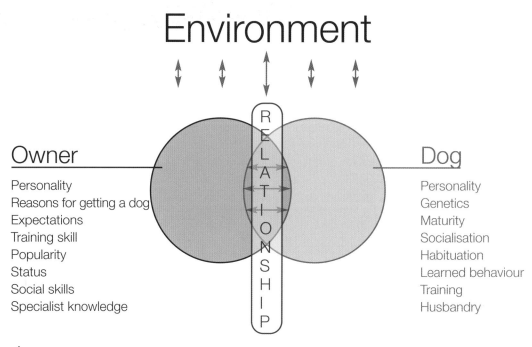

# Environment

## Owner

Personality
Reasons for getting a dog
Expectations
Training skill
Popularity
Status
Social skills
Specialist knowledge

## RELATIONSHIP

## Dog

Personality
Genetics
Maturity
Socialisation
Habituation
Learned behaviour
Training
Husbandry

*Diagnosing a relationship is difficult
because so many factors play a role.*

personalities, breed-specific potential and talents and the basic canine genetic configuration. In our part of the world, they usually grow up dependent on people. Their environment is as changeable and flexible as ours, which is why they are highly adaptable and equipped with complex learning behaviour.

Before a dog's problematic behaviour can be explained, we first have to be able to describe the individual partners that interact in this conflict situation and the environmental conditions. Indications of the potential for change can only be found in the communicative overlap between owners and dogs. After all, a problem only begins when somebody is aware of it and this is where people come into play. The person on the other end of the lead is doubtless not to blame for the difficulties, but he or she does play a part.

## How can we explain a complex system?

To begin with, we could look at the dog and his behaviour to find out what factors must have been present to cause his aggression. What motives guide him and how powerful is this motivation? What has the dog learned in the conflict? In terms of learning theory, what options are there for reducing his aggressive behaviour?

In the second step, we can examine the owner more closely. Why does this person have a dog? What function does the dog perform for its owner? What expectations does the owner have for the dog? What training goals are they pursuing? What kind of training style do they have? How do they react to the problem?

The relationship should be analysed in the third step. What basic patterns have developed in communication? Which rules have been established? How are conflicts dealt with in the partnership? What effects does the problem have on the relationship? What is perpetuating the problem? What has to change to make a solution possible?

## Conflict is important!

Aggressive behaviour is part of social communication. It is neither an illness nor dysfunctional, but helps to sort out conflicts in a group and to establish and maintain the rules of coexistence. Aggression can help you to assert yourself in a competitive situation, but also to protect yourself. It can therefore involve attack as well as defence, so it has an important function.

We humans are familiar with a dog's reasons for acting aggressively, because we have the same motives. What many people find strange is dogs' directness at expressing their feelings and attitudes. Adult humans are often more inhibited, not as spontaneous and frequently experience conflicts retrospectively, reflect on them and think about strategies for the next time. They are able to weave intrigue and to wage abstract wars. Dogs can't do that. They have a remarkable culture of conflict that is very impulsive and direct, similar to children. Dog training cannot be about taking dogs' way of arguing away from them just because we don't like it, but that doesn't mean that dogs can be unrestricted in their aggressive behaviour towards one another. We can help them to become integrated into society so that they

*Communication among dogs is direct and highly sophisticated.*
*This older dog uses his gaze and posture to communicate aggressively and the young dog gives the appropriate response with submissive behaviour. (Photo: Nadin Matthews)*

can be our companions in life. Aggression is part of this, but it can be demonstrated by dogs to an extent that is appropriate to the situation.

Dogs have and can learn rules for conflict. Most altercations between dogs are admittedly noisy, but bloodless and ritualised. If a dog gets bitten, it is usually a feeble bite with no intention to harm. Dogs are even able to demonstrate aggressive behaviour with subtle nuances, which do not have to be loud at all. Dogs use their body language, body tension, facial expression and gaze to inform others about a looming conflict.

# The dog and factors for aggressive behaviour

To begin by getting an overview, the factors for aggression have been listed individually. In real life, these factors tend to go hand-in-hand. Very seldom is taking one particular motive away from a dog enough to make him relax.

## Genetics

"Who am I supposed to be?"

As dog trainers, we often avoid public discussion about genetic factors in aggression so as not to further fan the flames of policy against dogs and, specifically, against certain breeds. It goes without saying that there are breed-specific differences. However, the dangerousness of a dog cannot be determined by its breed alone, but must always be considered individually.

Humans have bred more than 400 breeds of dog and you can find a problem with each one of them. If I don't like aggression, but I do enjoy the beauty of an athletic body that moves away from me quickly, then I am a hound person. If I enjoy conflict but have a small car, I would be best to get a Jack Russell Terrier. If I have a big car and a love of conflict, a Boerboel could enrich my life. If I have a great need for closeness and neighbours that would enjoy my dog's loud vocalisations at the start of a walk, a German Shepherd would be ideal. If the neighbours prefer things to be quieter and I like lonely walks, it could also be something special like a Shiba Inu. If, even after all these years, I still like Jennifer Grey's hairdo from *Dirty Dancing*, I could find a great friend in a poodle, with a little in the way of training. If

*Breed-specific characteristics can point towards the likelihood of aggressive behaviour occurring, but not to its actual occurrence. A Pointer will be tend to be more interested in hunting than in aggressive conflicts.*

I have a tendency to say "I'm sorry", because I know that my dog, despite his behaviour, will be met with sympathy, a retriever would be an excellent choice.

Basically, almost any dog is able to behave aggressively at the end of his lead.

However, breeds that tend to quickly go into a rage, become hysterical, be insecure or initially reject anything strange, have a greater chance of developing problems on the lead. In breed descriptions, the words brave, distrustful, agile, reserved and alert are usually used for these characteristics.

Breed-specific differences can increase the probability that aggressive behaviour will occur and give a crucial indication of how great a dog's willingness and ability is to stop this behaviour again. Defending his territory is definitely going to be more important to a livestock guarding dog than it is to a Maltese Terrier. The question of how motivated the dog is, along with other factors, will significantly determine the nature of training.

# Inadequate socialisation

"Who am I in 'us'?"

Socialisation describes the process whereby an individual dog comes to identify with a group or society and it is the result of social learning. It is a lifelong process, but it is still more important in some phases of life than in others. These stages of life are called sensitive phases. Puppyhood could be described as primary socialisation, where fundamental

*Young dogs need enough contact with other canines to learn how to communicate and to be able to assess other dogs. (Photo: Nadin Matthews)*

behaviour patterns and rules for individual communication are learnt. During juvenile or secondary socialisation, on the other hand, rules and norms are learned in a group and each individual's personality is developed through clashes with others, which is how dogs find their own place and role. Dogs need adequate opportunity to keep practising communication, for example, through play. This also includes aggressive communication. If a dog is never allowed to enter into conflict as a puppy, then he can't learn how to deal with aggression. However, that does not mean that the owner should just let everything take its course and never intervene. Young dogs need different amounts of help to be able to integrate into our society and that is what training, the conscious, methodical and deliberate part of socialisation, is for. However, we should not overestimate our abilities, as most of socialisation is fed by unintentional experiences that an individual gathers and that affect their personality. That means that husbandry conditions are crucial above all things, along with training considerations. If an individual has not been able to learn about communication adequately, they will not feel confident and secure in later life. Insecurity is a common motive for aggression.

## Self-image

"Me, myself and I."

On the dog scene, people like to talk a lot about dogs' privileges. It is said that, the more privileges a dog has, the more difficult

*Dogs' self-image comes from their personality and social feedback. Important dogs behave as if they are important.*

he will be. There are different ideas about what constitutes a privilege, for example, giving the dog too much attention and affection, raised or strategically important sleeping places, unlimited access to food or toys, letting the dog go through the door first and many more.

But does every dog perceive these things to be privileges and does this constitute status in a group? Will taking these things away from the dog solve everything? What makes statements like these difficult is that dogs and people are individuals. The statements could certainly apply to some dogs. Other dogs, however, have little interest in attention from their owners and enjoy getting some peace from them. Some would prefer to sleep on cold tiles in a dark corner because the sofa is too hot for them; some do not place any additional value on food or toys or on who goes through the door first; and some derive great enjoyment from all of these things, but still don't have any problems.

Nevertheless, nobody could deny that dogs glean information about their self-image from how they coexist. Who am I in the group? How do I see myself in relation to the others? These questions are constantly being answered in communication. Paul Watzlawick calls this the "relationship aspect", which is present in every exchange of information. The relationship information is usually in the "how" of a message and not in the "what". Self-image, feelings and attitudes towards others are primarily expressed through body language.

Accordingly, the status and also the role in the group are determined much more subtly, in my opinion, and are expressed accordingly. Relationships are not objective, but per-

ceptible. They are nourished by the sum of all of the emotional conditions that we experience in mutual communication and find expression in the mood of the group. But who actually determines the mood? Whose mood is the basis for the group behaviour? Who in the group reassures the others that their mood is appropriate? Who is allowed to change whose mood? Maybe it is not so much a question of how important the dog considers himself to be, but rather how seriously we take ourselves as people. Have we learned to adapt to others' moods? The dog will pick up on this and will probably take charge, becoming accustomed to seeing his own mood as the deciding one.

You could say that the owner looks to their dog for guidance. Being able to set the mood in a pack is a great privilege; it directs the group, entails a lot of responsibility and identifies the pack member that makes the important decisions. For dogs, this doesn't have to be about the conscious use of power at all. Rather, it is obvious for them that they can behave according to their mood and they expect their owner to do the same, following the maxim: 'Now we are happy and exuberant; now we are sleepy and quiet; now we are excited and frantic; now we are aggressive; now we are uncertain; now we are cuddly and affectionate.' That does not mean that the dog questions the status of his owner and aggressively asserts themselves against them. It just means that the owner's influence in important situations, for example, when meeting other dogs, decreases, because the dog does not feel compelled to ask his owner or to seek guidance from them. The dog uses the owner's feelings as the basis. Don't get me wrong. It makes sense to empathise with your dog and to consider his needs, but the question of who fundamentally determines the mood within the system can be important when difficulties arise.

## Frustration

"It's not my party if I'm not allowed to dance."

If somebody is frustrated, their physiologically measurable state of excitement becomes heightened. According to psychoanalyst John S. Dollard, frustration occurs when someone is disrupted in their purposeful activity and cannot perform it. One option for letting off steam and, as a result, returning to your normal emotional state is to act aggressively. Giving vent to your anger brings palpable relief. This liberating feeling is then learned and aggression can become a strategy for gaining relief from an unpleasant state of excitement. You have perhaps experienced what happens when a purposeful activity is interrupted when you want to drive home from work after a long day and are stuck in traffic. Wild horn honking, gesticulating and banging on the steering wheel are examples of behaviours that help people to cope while waiting in a queue.

Some readers will be nodding now and recognising themselves in that situation, while others won't, because they are much more patient and casually wait in their car without becoming frustrated. It actually takes different people different lengths of time to become frustrated. On the one hand, this is to do with individual temperament and

*If a dog isn't used to restrictions, he will struggle to cope with them and quickly become frustrated.*

character and, on the other, with individual learning experiences. It is the same for dogs.

If dogs are never allowed to walk without a lead, are not kept occupied and are only taken for a walk outside for ten minutes, it is no surprise that they become frustrated and behave aggressively as a result. The solution to the problem is obvious – the dog needs more exercise. But what about dogs that are well exercised, that have been allowed to run free a lot from a young age, have seldom had to wait and whose needs are always satisfied immediately? What do they need? The answer is frustration tolerance. They have not learned to tolerate slight delays in satisfaction of need and, as a result, they experience frustration early when they are confronted with minor limitations. This can also include walking on the lead. Dogs that yap at the end of the lead out of frustration do not usually have a problem with other dogs, but with not being able to get to the other dog because of the restriction of the lead.

Perhaps it's just a personal feeling, but I have the impression that, in the face of much early intervention in children as well as puppies, we increasingly forget to give them the right training in being patient, waiting and tolerating limitations. These skills would protect them from becoming frustrated, because frustration will inevitably come. Children should be able to sit quietly in school by six at the oldest and dogs should be able to accompany their owners everywhere and behave quietly, even if life tempts or even provokes them. To be able to do this, they need a healthy tolerance for frustration. Incidentally, experiments have shown that other strategies also help to relieve the state of excitement that results from frustration, for example, conversations or even laughter – just a little tip for your next traffic jam.

# Puberty

## "Too many hormones; not enough brain"

In the course of their individual development, dogs go through sensitive phases during which the brain grows, the neural network becomes denser and learning is more pronounced and long-lasting. Puppyhood is one of these phases and it is the foundation for the development of the adult dog. Much has been written and discussed about this topic in the dog world. Attending a puppy training group is now compulsory for dog owners in Germany. Unlike the puppy phase, puberty in dogs is seldom described as pleasant by their owners. Dogs become more headstrong and unapproachable, their world expands, their interest becomes more directed to the outside and, in the process, they forget what they have already learned and sometimes their good upbringing.

If you ask people when problems with lead aggression began in their dog, the answer is often that the dog was between eight and sixteen months old. Coincidence? No, because puberty is also a sensitive phase. Brain researchers even call it a second birth. Even though it cannot be seen in adolescent dogs and people, the brain is developing to a great extent during this time. The brain is being restructured or you could even say "closed for alterations"!

*Young dogs may not know what they're doing, but they do it with great enthusiasm.*

The frontal lobe of the brain only enters a stable and developed state at the end of puberty, following the tumultuous growth phase and it is one of the last areas of the brain to do so. This part of the brain is responsible for weighing up impulses, which, in people, we call reason. Therefore, dogs may find it very hard to resist impulses during puberty. They react more impulsively to emotional impressions than adult dogs do. Young male dogs, in particular, have an even bigger battle with their hormones. Their testosterone tells them that they are a real man and that is how they walk around their neighbourhood. They also find it difficult to assess how others are expressing their feelings and often get involved in conflicts because of their exaggerated behaviour and the inability to judge other dogs correctly.

This turbulent time is sometimes difficult for dog owners. They have to act as a replacement brain for their dog, be consistent and, despite their young dog's intensely fluctuating emotions, quietly and confidently insist that rules are followed and help their dog to react appropriately to impressions. This is a big responsibility. If you just pick up on all of your dog's behaviour like an old schoolmaster and focus on the temporarily confused, often insecure and senseless dog, then he won't have many options other than to act in an undesirable manner. Puberty is just a phase, but the experiences gathered during this phase remain in the memory for a long time. Can you still remember back to then? To the privilege of being young?

## Status

"It's lonely at the top."

Status-related aggression is usually a problem within the family and is fortunately rare. The term describes a situation where the dog is

*When dogs become too much for their owners, aggression on the lead is the least of the worries. (Photo: Nadin Matthews)*

dominant over its owner and controls him or her, but does not allow itself to be controlled.

The normal allocation of roles comes apart at the seams. The human is still the provider, but the dog determines the rules of coexistence to a large extent. If the person accepts this over a longer period, the self-image of both manifests itself. Aggression always results when the human resists the restrictions or tries to physically restrain the dog in this situation. If your dog threatens you in the home, does not always allow you to enter certain rooms, or if you cannot hold your dog by the collar, care for him or stop him from doing something because he will bite you, then aggression on the lead is the least of your worries. You have an entirely different problem. Get help!

*Lead aggression is almost always socially motivated. (Photo: Nadin Matthews)*

## Social partner

"Friendship!"

Dogs are social animals and, in our part of the world, they usually grow up dependent on people, sometimes forming very close bonds with their owners. This is unusual between two different species. We can take our adult, sexually mature dog to a park where other dogs are walked and let him off his lead there, where he meets other members of his own species. He could get to know another dog, fall in love, move out and start his own family. This is something that we rarely hear about, with the exception of when bitches are on heat. Because, when the owner walks in the direction of the car,

making it clear that it is time to go home, the dog leaves the other dogs and runs along behind his owner.

However, as is so often the case, there is another side to the coin. The dog's social need for closeness to people, to be seen and appraised by them, can turn into monopolisation. That means that the dog begins to defend his owner against other dogs or even people. If the owner is the reason for the aggression, aggression can normally also be observed when the dog is off the lead. Dogs try to keep others at a distance from their human, block their way, shove between them and briefly attack them. Socially motivated aggression works nowhere better than on the lead, because nobody really has to get into a fight. The lead protects the dog. How many dogs would put their head above the parapet if they really had to carry out their threat? Hardly any. But in the security of being held by their owner, some animals tend to overestimate their own abilities. Their owner on the other end of the lead gives them both the necessary security and a reason to act aggressively. Dogs whose aggression is socially motivated are peaceful or even lost without their owner. Try out the following test with your dog:

TEST

Tie up your dog to a tree or post and stand next to him. Ask another dog owner to approach you and stand in front of your dog. If your dog starts to pull on the lead and bark, walk away behind your dog and observe his reaction. Does he keep barking at the other dog or does he look for you behind him?

**A**
He looks for me and only starts barking at the other dog again when I approach him.

**B**
Despite several repetitions, it does not matter to him whether I stand next to him or move away. He still keeps barking at the other dog.

If he behaves as described under A, your presence is a crucial motive for your dog's aggression. If he behaves as described under B, he has other reasons for this behaviour or has already learned it.

## Sexuality

"Most murders don't happen because of love, but because of jealousy."

Is it really always about "the One"? No, but it often is. Aggressive behaviour is more common towards members of the same sex. Because of the biological need to reproduce, representatives of the same gender become competitors in the battle to conquer a member or members of the other gender. The aim of imposing behaviour is to demonstrate the individual's strengths and to impress both the object of desire and the competition.

*When it comes to reproduction,
many dogs surpass themselves.
(Photo: Nadin Matthews)*

Male dogs tend to display this behaviour more than bitches and get involved in sexually motivated quarrels more frequently. Do I really have to mention at this point that the same phenomenon can be observed in any bar on a Saturday night? Conquer, protect and defend. It happens every day and is the basis for many crime novels where a murder because of jealousy is a popular theme.

The power of hormones can be seen in the behaviour of the male dogs in a neighbourhood when a bitch is on heat. Many dogs are castrated, which adds to the hormonal "confusion". Uncastrated males get into confrontations over castrated dogs and bitches may well see castrated males as competition. That does not mean that castration doesn't make sense once in a while, just that there are also downsides to our intervention in dogs' sexuality.

Dogs may defend people, as well as other dogs, for sexual reasons. Dogs know the difference between male and female owners. Hormonal changes in people can correspondingly influence aggressive behaviour. So women have been fighting to get rid of jealous males for years and now the dog starts? The good thing is that dogs are easier to control so that the relationship doesn't have to end. Please, keep hold of your male dog. We can help you!

# Territory

"Wherever people put up fences, dogs stand behind them and bark."

Dogs are territorial animals. A territory is an area that is defended against intruders to protect both food and young. Dogs usually mark their territory through smell, for example, by scent marking. People, on the other hand, mark their territory optically, for example, using boundaries, walls or garden fences. But does a territory really end at the garden fence? Not for dogs. Their territory can also include the driveway, the street, the typical walk route or their own car. Furthermore, it does not take a dog long to make an area its own territory. My dogs take exactly two hours to call a holiday apartment their own. I need just ten minutes. I make similar territorial claims within a five-metre radius

*Dogs often lay territorial claims to their regular walking routes.*

of my towel on the beach, at a table in a café, on a park bench or in a place where I am standing. People are like that and so are dogs. The question is about the intensity with which the aggression is expressed. After all, I don't stab somebody to death just because they come and sit with me at the table, but you would see my discomfort in my body language. The aggression is present, but in-hibited, and inhibition is something that can be learned. Neighbourhood disputes that end up in court show how territorial aggression can get out of control. Yet we are surprised when our dog tries to start a fight with the neighbour's dog. How strange.

*Even when dogs aren't hungry, food can still spark quarrels about ownership.*

Take your dog somewhere that is un-familiar to him. Does he behave less ag-gressively on his lead? Then territory plays an important role.

## Food

"Only children don't share?!"

On the one hand, food is a good way of rewarding your dog for the desired behaviour, but, on the other hand, your dog may defend this very food against other dogs. And if that is the case, can you never take food with you on a walk? No, you just have to teach the dog that he is not allowed to defend it.

To find out whether food is actually a factor in the dog's aggression, it makes sense to walk without taking along food for a week. Does this make the dog more relaxed with other dogs? If so, then food could be a motive.

For us, it's a game with a ball;
for some dogs, it's a serious hunt.

# Prey

## "Freshly caught rubber ball"

From a genetic point of view, dogs and humans are hunters. Once upon a time, prey was something that you could eat. Nowadays, neither dogs nor people go hunting in the classic sense, to kill to eat. However, predisposition to hunt has not disappeared as a result of this; it is just expressed in a different way. Sport is a popular substitute for giving expression to our motivation to hunt and so is shopping. First you catch your prey and then you defend it. Have you ever tried to steal a bag of freshly caught shoes from a female? Don't do it, because it could end badly – and bloodily – for you. This form of aggression is called "prey aggression". Of course, you can't eat shoes and you can't eat a ball either, but they can still be captured and defended. Evidence of this can be found every Saturday on sports programmes and every day where people walk their dogs.

People actually have a talent for expanding their dog's prey spectrum with their own preferences. How do we do that? We pick up an object, wave it back and forth quickly, throw it and let the dog chase it. The dog chases the object, grabs it, shakes it and enjoys his little moment of hunting success. For people, it's a game and a toy; for some dogs, it's a hunt and prey. And prey can be defended. It's strange that a dog can be bitten by another over a rubber ball, simply because somebody had previously made this ball into prey. However, it is also strange that safety precautions for a football match equal those of an important state visit. In a similar way

to food-motivated aggression, it could be enough that a high-value toy is in the owner's jacket pocket on the walk.

Do not take any toys on your walk for a week and do not react to the dog when he drops a stick at your feet.
Does this make the dog more relaxed with other dogs? Then prey is a motive for his aggressive behaviour.

# Stress

## "Burn-out?"

Who doesn't know that feeling? You've had a stressful day and you are irritable. Sometimes it just takes the proverbial straw to break the donkey's back. If someone says the wrong thing or makes the wrong gesture you flip out – completely understandable. Readiness to attack increases because large amounts of the stress hormone corticosterone are released and the consequence is that you fly off the handle. Aggression can be caused by stress. Nowadays, people often suffer from stress, and burn-out has become a widespread disease. For more and more people, life is characterised by rapid change and pressure, without the necessary support or grounding from family, religion and work.

The resulting anxiety exceeds many people's natural capacity to adapt.

But what about dogs? Things can also get too much for them so that they lose their rag if they constantly have to perform, always have to meet expectations, are put under pressure and, at the same time, get too little quiet time and freedom. Furthermore, they also do not have the chance to escape when they are on the lead. If this is the case, it is important to find out what keeps stressing the dog. It's easy if the stressors can be avoided or if the stress can be counteracted by more peace and freedom, but it becomes more difficult if this is not the case. The dog has to learn to deal with stress better in the long term. Long-term stress is both the physical basis as well as the consequence of many mental difficulties and it is closely linked to anxiety and also trauma, so serious stress problems clearly require treatment.

However, another question needs to be asked before making this diagnosis. Is the dog actually under stress, or does the owner perhaps suffer from stress and brings his or her own mental overload into the relationship? Many people suffer from exhaustion and stress-related disorders. They tend to project their emotional state onto the dog and perhaps perceive their dog to be stressed because they are. Perhaps the dog also takes on the mood of the owner. Recommending

*Stress is an unpleasant physiological state and can provide a breeding ground for aggression. (Photo: Nadin Matthews)*

that that the dog experiences less stress could have unfortunate consequences. For people suffering from stress, it is extremely important that the dog and the daily walk do not become something else that they need to work on and, what's more, it would be the wrong thing to work on.

# Insecurity

"When you don't know
how you should behave."

Social insecurity can promote aggressive behaviour. If you do not feel secure, you will quickly feel threatened and tend towards misinterpretation and making the wrong decisions. On the lead, the result is something that looks, sounds and feels the same as any other lead aggression. (The pain in your shoulder is the same, after all.)

The difference tends to be noticeable when the dog is running free. The very same dog that had just seemed so determined on the lead, barking a very direct "I'll kill you, you swine" at the other dog, suddenly no longer seems as convincing off the lead and his conversation is more along the lines of "That wasn't me before, that was my brother" or "Oh, I didn't recognise you for a minute there. And how are you?"

Insecure dogs are usually only heroes when they are on the lead. When they are running free, on the other hand, they tend to look for victims that had behaved like victims before to enhance the status of their personality. But they aren't bad and, even if they were, they still deserve sympathy, because

*If a dog doesn't feel confident in communicating with others, he may tend to overreact.*

35

they need aggressive behaviour to get the situation under control so that they can feel secure.

Therefore, the crucial question is what is making the dog insecure? Is it himself, perhaps because he is going through puberty or because he is ill? Or is it his owner, because he does not act decisively or give him any direction, but leaves the decisions to him? Or has he had a bad experience with other dogs?

Insecurity should not be confused with anxiety. Unlike an anxious dog, an insecure dog has more room to manoeuvre within his strategies. Anxious dogs are forced to make a decision; insecure dogs make the decision themselves. Anxious dogs feel like they are fighting for their life; insecure dogs are only fighting for control and structure.

If you offer an insecure dog more security, he will usually gladly accept. For this type of dog, social support leads to resolution of an unpleasant situation. Unfortunately, it is not that easy with anxious dogs, but then they don't bark loudly at the end of the lead when another dog approaches them.

*Anxious dogs first seek refuge in flight.*

## Anxiety

"The eternal retreat."

Ask somebody with a phobia of spiders or snakes how they act when they catch sight of the object of their fear. You can guarantee that this person will not fix their gaze on the snake or spider from 50 metres away and imposingly march right up to it before provoking it at close proximity and loud volume. A dog that is afraid of other dogs wouldn't act like that either.

Fear is the primary emotion of stress and is expressed by the desire for avoidance, among other things. The physical symptoms of anxiety, such as a racing heart and trembling, are unpleasant. A fearful dog will not pull on the lead in the direction of an approaching dog, but will attempt to flee as soon as he sees it. He will only aggressively defend himself if he can no longer flee and is distressed by the other dog. He will dart forward to bite quickly, with his body low to the ground, flattened ears and clamped tail, before withdrawing again. Dogs that are really afraid of other dogs need therapeutic help and definitely not training for aggression on the lead.

# Trauma

"Ignorance doesn't have
to make you blind."

Caspar lived in a small kennel for eight years and was only very seldom walked through the village on a short lead. He only had contact with other dogs as a puppy. The permanent restriction of movement with no escape left its mark. He exhibited stereotypical behaviour in the kennel because of neglect and lack of exercise. For long periods of the day, he jumped approximately 2 metres up the fence from a standing position. Badam, badam, badam, short break, and then it began again. On his short, rare walks, he panicked whenever he met another dog. He was so frustrated and stressed that he displayed his aggression with great intensity, advancing, drooling, spinning round, biting his lead and shooting forward again. This behaviour was also stereotypical and had a recognisable rhythm.

*Mental health problems are becoming more common in dogs too, and the time has come for new approaches in behavioural therapy. (Photo: Nadin Matthews)*

When Caspar was eight years old, his owner died and the collie went to the dogs' home. When he arrived, he continued to behave as normal. He showed his typical patterns in the kennel as well as on the lead. The animal shelter decided to try integrating Caspar into a pack of dogs. He was now used to wearing a muzzle and all safety precautions had been taken for the day of integration. He was let into the enclosure with the other dogs and the concerns turned out to be unfounded. Caspar made contact with the other dogs, interacted with them appropriately, was even able to communicate with other males with inhibited aggression and quickly found his place within the group. He behaved completely normally. The only time Caspar didn't join in was when the pack reacted aggressively to dogs walking by the fence, whereupon he reverted back to his old patterns and jumped up at the fence stereotypically. The animal shelter had hoped that, because of his new lifestyle that involved sufficient contact with other dogs and enough to keep him occupied, Caspar would change his behaviour on the lead. However, lead aggression remained a part of his daily walks. In his behaviour, he did not distinguish between male or female, castrated dogs or puppies.

As we have said, Caspar was good natured inside the enclosure, even if people were in there dealing with all the dogs. But whenever anybody tried to put Caspar on a lead and take him out of the enclosure for a walk, something strange happened to him. As soon as the lead was clipped onto his collar, Caspar's behaviour basically changed and he immediately wanted to attack the next available dog, even if he had been inter-acting amiably with that same dog before.

If you look at Caspar's history, it immediately becomes clear that his behaviour is not normal aggression. If he were a person, the word "trauma" would come to mind.

A psychological trauma is a life-threatening event that creates extreme mental strain and leads to a sensory overload. Trauma can result from physical or emotional abuse, but also isolation and neglect. Unlike a bad experience or normal grief, the affected person cannot process the trauma. The brain stores a traumatic event in a place that is not readily accessible for revaluation. This means that the trauma has not gone, but works from the "background", causing many psychological problems. Possible consequences are insomnia and depression, but also anxiety, excessive irritability, anger and antisocial behaviour. People who have been traumatised also do not have any control over their impulses. Helplessness and anger are very closely linked. Fragmented recollections such as a certain smell, a certain image, a sight or a sound can become a trigger for reliving the trauma.

There are many traumatised people in Germany and treatment options are many and varied. Currently, there is very little specialist knowledge about traumatised dogs and their behaviour, but lots of things from the world of humans can be applied to dogs. If a dog displays sporadic outbursts of aggression that do not correspond to the situation when looked at objectively and trauma cannot be ruled out from his history, you should start thinking along these lines. As with anxiety, therapeutic help is also required for trauma, even if help in this area is scarce.

# Illness

"The limitations of dog training."

Acute as well as chronic disease can drastically change a dog's behaviour. Pain, itching and internal upsets, for example, caused by allergies, changes in the hormone system or diseases of the organs can cause aggression as well as other behavioural changes.

When an adult dog suddenly becomes aggressive for no discernable reason, it is often an indication of acute suffering. If your dog's behaviour spontaneously changes like this, your first port of call should be your vet, not a dog trainer. Without your help, diagnosis is not always easy for the vet. You know your dog better than anybody. Have you noticed that he reacts more sensitively to some forms of contact, limps more often, scratches more than usual at certain times of the year, drinks more than normal, is suddenly less confident than before or is behaving differently at the moment? There are different experts for different topics within the field of medicine. Along with general and specialist vets, it may be worth visiting alternative practitioners, homeopaths, osteopaths or animal physiotherapists.

In the case of chronic disease, you and the specialists involved should look at the extent to which training the dog is possible. Sometimes this is a cost-benefit analysis, because the strain that the dog undergoes because of his aggressive behaviour or by pulling on the lead can be greater than the strain that the dog would experience during the training phase.

*The way we breed dogs aids the development of mental and physical illness.*

# Environmental influences

"What's on the outside
makes what's on the inside."

Dogs don't just get feedback from their owners but also from the environment. For example, people will judge a big, black dog and a small, light-coloured dog differently. People treat dogs differently in the country

*Times are still hard for some breeds.*
*(Photo: Nadin Matthews)*

compared with in the city, because population density determines the freedom dogs can be given. Dogs have to be registered by law and dog ownership is subject to certain rules. All of these things influence the human-dog relationship and therefore the behaviour of the dog.

An example from the year 2000 shows the effect that even a small change in environmental conditions can have. There was a terrible incident where a child was killed by a Staffordshire Bull Terrier in Hamburg. Subsequently, a new regulation meant that all Staffis had to be walked with a lead and muzzle. Of course, there was no time to get the dogs used to a muzzle properly and they dealt with it badly as a result. Dogs that had been used to running free and playing with other dogs were now walked past them on the lead. Out of fear for their children, people heckled these so-called fighting dogs

and their owners on the street. The press had also found their bogeyman and did their usual. There was actually only a small legal change, but it had a major impact on the human-dog system involved and significantly affected the behaviour of the dogs.

## Learned behaviour

"When behaviour no longer
needs a reason."

When a dog no longer needs his original reason to act aggressively, we call it learned aggression.

Let's take the example of territorial and sexually motivated aggression. Female dogs Layla and Kira agree on one thing: they don't like each other. Their respective gardens are just 200 metres apart. Kira's owners do not have any other option than to walk past Layla's garden when they go for their daily walk. When Layla is in the garden and Kira walks past on her lead on the other side of the fence, they both show what they're made of. Regina Halmich would be impressed. People were afraid that they would tear each other apart if the fence hadn't been there. When the whole thing started, Kira would leave her garden in a normal mood and only started to show aggression when she saw Layla. That was a long time ago. Now she ruffles up her feathers at her own front door and pulls on her lead on the way to Layla's garden, panting audibly as she does so. As she gets closer to the site of the conflict, her breathing takes on a slightly hysterical undertone and one or two barks slip out. The showdown begins when she reaches the other dog's garden fence. Kira has developed expectations, which is an important aspect when aggression is learned. In this case, her learning is situational, i.e. her mood is linked to the location and the sight of the garden fence becomes the trigger. But the story doesn't end there, because even if Layla isn't in the garden, Kira practically tries to start a fight with fresh air at the garden fence. She no longer needs Layla as a stimulus; the garden fence is enough. That is the result of a learning process. It would be interesting if Layla and all of her family moved out and a new family moved in with their dog. There is a good chance that Kira would hate this dog too.

*Learned aggression is triggered by new stimuli that were acquired during the original conflict.*

People and their role

# in aggressive behaviour

As you have perhaps already established, giving a professional description of the factors for a dog's behaviour is a major project in itself, but things get really complicated when you add the owner into the mix. Because, when people these days talk about their dogs, it becomes clear how closely they coexist together and how few differences there are when compared with human relationships. Dogs have sneaked their way first into our homes and then into our hearts. The relationship between people and dogs can no longer be explained by domestication alone.

Apart from a few rare working dogs or pure status symbols, dogs live with us in a family group, even though they are members of a different species. If we look at it objectively, it is easier to find reasons not to have a dog than to have a one. They do not have any obvious usefulness, they don't always smell nice, they have parasites, we have to support them, they need veterinary care and they often misbehave. In the course of its life, a German dog costs an average of ⇔10,000.00 to keep. We are happy to pay and accept anything that comes along. Not just because we are exceptionally nice people, but because we need dogs to fulfil our emotional needs. The reasons for getting a dog can be many and varied and, to a large extent, they lay the foundations for the relationship between owner and dog.

# Reasons for getting a dog and expectations

The great thing about dogs is that they basically provide a projection screen for every-thing. They can help people not to feel lonely or even to get to know other people. They can bring greater commitment to human pair bonds, acting as a child or grandchild substitute. They can constitute part of a leisure activity or be an element of nature that you bring into the home. They never leave home even when they are adults and you can worry about them, pet them and look after them. You can use them to express and emphasise your own personality and give full expression to your feelings. You can bring up a dog as you were raised or do everything better. Dogs protect people who are nervous. Sometimes they are also an extension of the self and behave as people would never dare to behave. However, today's reasons for getting a dog also shape its role in the group. For example, people get dogs for comfort after a separation or during a change of life where somebody wants more time and space for their own needs. This includes the long-cherished desire to finally have a dog. The dog may then be entrusted with the task of expressing the new-found feeling of freedom and making it palpable for the owner.

The dog's purpose will determine how he and his owner communicate together. His function goes hand-in-hand with expectations of him and can even determine the way the dog is trained. For example, some people try to use the dog to make up for everything that hasn't worked out for them before, or they find in the dog somebody to whom they can show their strength, somebody who will listen to them. This is not meant to be a judgement, but an illustration of how individual the human-dog relationship can be.

Role allocation even lies behind how people consider their dog's needs. For example,

*People have certain expectations for their dogs and make their choices accordingly.*

some owners feel that their dog prefers to sit indoors on the sofa and doesn't really need to run around much. Others put themselves under immense pressure because they believe that dogs constantly need to be kept occupied and active to feel good. Similar differences of opinion arise on questions about feeding, toys, medical care and, above all, training.

However, problems with the dog cannot simply be explained by the dog's behaviour and cannot be changed just by working on the dog alone.

# When expectations are not met

Let's take a scene from a puppy group as a clear and simple example. People, who are actually not relevant to this story, meet through their dogs every Saturday at a fenced-in field. There they stand, young and old, tall and short, with their different dogs, who momentarily all have one thing in common: they are all sort of cute and ex-

*Dogs have personalities and minds of their own. They cannot be forced into every role people choose for them. (Photo: Nadin Matthews)*

uberant and the little girls, who have come along to the puppy group holding their mum's hand, keep shouting "Isn't he cute?!" It goes without saying that everybody actually likes their own dog best. How could it be any other way? But, nevertheless, the people who make the pilgrimage to the group every weekend could hardly be more different. They had different reasons for getting a dog and their expectations are sometimes miles apart.

One family had bought a Labrador puppy, because they wanted the kids to grow up with a dog and be able to play with it. The parents are looking forward to taking the dog for walks in the country. The family now seems complete: parents, two children and a playful Labrador Retriever. The reason for getting the dog already implies the parents' expectations for it, namely, that it should be good natured. That is the main duty of a family dog, which is understandable from the point of view of a family. From a genetic point of view, a retriever is also a dog. They are bred to retrieve the kill while hunting and are mainly used for hunting ducks. On the one hand, they are supposed to be eager to please but, on the other hand, physically robust and independent. Their potential for aggression can be considered to be low in comparison with many other breeds. In terms of breed, the family hasn't made a bad choice.

Another member of the puppy group is a hunter with a German Hunting Terrier. In later life, the puppy is to be used for hunting wild boar, foxes and badgers and he already has the necessary skills for this. As a terrier, he is able to become involved in a hunting situation without requiring a leader and to attack an animal bigger than himself. If this animal defends itself by attacking the terrier, the terrier will not run away but will switch from hunting mode into aggressive behaviour. Without exaggerating, you could say that a German Hunting Terrier has high potential for aggression in comparison to a Labrador. The hunter is not only prepared for this; the potential for aggression actually describes his expectations for his little companion.

A short exercise follows that aims to make sure that the dog will allow prey it has found to be taken away from it, in an emergency. The trainer throws a chew stick into the circle. The puppies are allowed to chew on it and, after a few minutes, the handlers are supposed to try to take the prey away from the puppy, while it is on its lead. First it's the turn of the family with the Labrador. They do not expect to have a problem and so approach their puppy with the lead slack. The puppy seems very happy with his chew stick and tries to keep hold of it, jumping to the side when his owners attempt to approach him. The family repeat this several times and, each time, the puppy keeps the prey. At least somebody is learning something. Then they shorten the lead and reach their dog and the chew stick, but when they try to take it away, the puppy makes a little sound that is commonly known as growling. What happens now is crucial. The family may shrink away because they did not expect this. At just ten weeks old, the Labrador is behaving aggressively, contrary to their expectations, and is being successful at it. Because of this, they could avoid the situation with the chew stick in future, so as not to be confronted with the wrong picture

*People often have greater difficulties dealing with aggression than dogs.*

again or they could react with frustration and anger and blow the whole thing out of proportion, therefore judging the dog's feeble attempt on an emotional level. The importance of the behaviour for the dog can also be gauged from this.

Now it's the turn of the hunter and his terrier. He knows about his dog's capabilities and would probably be disappointed if the little one was friendly in this situation. On the other hand, he also knows that the dog has to learn not to behave aggressively towards him, so he enters into the confrontation differently from the outset. He pulls his puppy towards him on the lead, grabs hold of him so that he can't get bitten and unapologetically picks up the chew stick. He nips the terrier's attempts to resist in the bud, then smiles about it and feels happy about his little dog's tenacity. After all, that is how he wants him to be.

Two completely different reactions to similar behaviour: the dogs will also learn different things as a result. So, following this chain of thought, the Labrador, with his genetically low tendency towards aggression, could develop food aggression in the future, while the German Hunting Terrier may have no future problems in this area. The genetic potential and the individual reasons for a dog to be aggressive are not crucial alone. The reasons for getting a dog, the expectations of the dog and the training style of the owners also play an important role.

# People's reactions and feelings

A person's attitudes are reflected in the feelings that they have in relation to the problem and in the reactions that they present to their dog as a result. After all, it's just a dog barking at the end of a lead. Where is the problem? There isn't one! We could be proud of our dogs; after all, it's a courageous feat. Some people see it as such and do not feel that there is a problem. Others are troubled by it and they represent the majority.

But why do people make conflicts between dogs their problem? This kind of transfer does not happen with all animals. At night, when I hear a strange cat trying to set foot in our garden but being attacked vociferously by our cat, I think something along the lines of "Well, that's just how it is." However, I would not be as calm if one our dogs lunged at another dog like that. Not because I think fights between dogs are bad, but because I see myself as being responsible. How my cats behave is not my business, but how my dogs behave is. Perhaps this is also linked to the role of the dog. We see dogs as products of our training and as a mirror of our attitudes to life. People may experience correspondingly powerful feelings when their dogs are aggressive on the lead. They may feel anxious, helpless and powerless, disappointed, angry or embarrassed. Sometimes a pet dog has a bigger emotional influence on a person than other people do. In turn, these emotions influence the behaviour of the dog, keep the vicious cycle going or even create new endless cycles. Dogs don't necessarily have a problem with aggression, but people do. How you deal with aggression yourself determines, to a great extent, the anguish that results when your dog behaves accordingly on the lead.

## Anger and guilt

The owner of Ben from our first case study is anxious, helpless and frustrated, which makes her a potential candidate for "going on the rampage". The nightly laps with the fear of meeting other male dogs take their toll. But don't worry, no one will really get hurt when she snaps, other than her and her relationship with her dog. Her previous conflict strategies have not proved to be successful.

She tries the same thing every time, but never achieves her goal. She is really very patient, but she is only human and her feelings about the problem are intense. When she has been trying for weeks to stop Ben from acting like a rowdy hooligan at the end of his lead, the day may come when frustration and stress gain the upper hand and she snaps. Days like this are usually different from others with regard to the dog owner's personal state of mind. They are days when everything goes wrong, when their back hurts or when there have already been problems in other aspects of life and when nerves are frayed. And then all of the pointless weeks of training add up. She has said "no" a hundred times and a hundred times the dog has misunderstood and it's the same again today. For the dog, the owner's reaction is sudden, almost out of the blue. This time, she doesn't care if people are looking; this time, the anger she has been bottling up drives her (remember frustration-related aggression?). The familiar situation arises and, once again, the familiar prevention strategies are unsuccessful, so she shouts at him in a way that neither of them has ever heard before. She turns towards him, harshly yanks him back on the lead, grabs his fur and screams. Ben gets the fright of his life and immediately responds with humility. He makes himself small and cowers as if he were beaten every day of his life. It is this sight that stops her and she is fully aware of what has just happened. She lost control, flipped out, overreacted and was unfair. She has learned that you don't do that and takes this feeling home with her. The mood is now characterised by guilt; she feels bad. And at home, she sits with Ben on the kitchen floor, cries into his fur, tells him she's sorry and promises never to do it again. She will keep this promise for a while, until it all gets too much again. It is the start of an endless cycle and a good time to make an appointment at the dog training school.

# Who do you meet at dog training?

We dog trainers are actually people. Like everybody else, we have also had experience of relationships and training and developed personal attitudes to these fundamental issues in life. After all, we have all been educated. We have all experienced different types of relationships and are part of this society and of the social, political and also economic system.

We may have been given too much or too little love and developed our individual need for closeness and distance on this basis. We may have a lot of or no experience with mental or physical violence and, for example, have derived fear of aggression or a highly developed need for power as a result. Perhaps we have lost trust in people or don't trust dogs. Perhaps we have a problem when people are weak towards their dogs or frequently assert themselves. We might also love freedom or need a lot of control in our lives. Perhaps we are desperate for recognition or want to please everybody. Perhaps we have learned that we always have to be strong and that everything must always happen very fast. In any case, we have different strengths and weaknesses when it comes to dealing with people and dogs, in building relationships and in training. Any approach in dog training says something about the trainer themselves, about their personal story and their ability to reflect upon themselves. We all want to help. Some of us want to help dogs, some of us want to help people, some of us want to help both and some maybe just want to help themselves.

And that is how dog owners and trainers meet. They tell us their stories. However, the interpretation of their and their dog's behaviour, the diagnosis of the problem and the training suggestions given are not made by an impartial agency but by us. This is based on our theories and methods, previous experiences and attitudes, strengths and weaknesses, specialist knowledge and intellectual position. Everybody has their own truth and, correspondingly, there are different statements and approaches, depending on where you are going.

*On closer examination, it becomes clear that discussions in dog training are more emotional than technical.*

Some of these training approaches can quickly be scientifically refuted, others have not been investigated, but most of them are a matter of attitude and opinion. Correspondingly, we cannot make judgements about right and wrong, but should discuss the appropriateness in each individual case. After all, when we are advising people about a problem with their dog, we are entering very personal territory. Apart from the fact that they all have a dog, there is no other way to define dog owners as a target group. We encounter many different feelings, attitudes to training and training styles, different life plans, living situations, family set-ups and different personalities that are connected to one another.

If you look at dog trainers' suggestions for resolving conflict, there are not as many approaches as it would initially appear. There are just many different names and different rationales. But the different approaches in training consultation are not the problem; the problem is the diagnoses! Or, to put it another way, all dog trainers are right, just not all the time.

If dog trainers commit themselves to a certain method, they tend to make their diagnoses according to this method. So, in some dog training clubs, you will tend to come across one of the following diagnoses more so than others when it comes to the topic of lead aggression:

1. The dog is afraid.
2. The dog is in charge.
3. The dog doesn't have enough to keep it occupied.
4. The dog is under stress.

Perhaps the diagnosis is correct, but perhaps it was a foregone conclusion. The last chapter covered factors for aggression and dealt with reasons for buying a dog and expectations for that dog. Hopefully, you will have recognised yourself and your dog at some point and have been able to find out more about your situation as a result.

Check for yourself which of the behavioural diagnoses fit you and your dog best, because you are and always will be the expert when it comes to you and your dog. You are not to blame for your dog's behaviour, but you are responsible for his training and therefore for what he experiences. Challenge your mind and listen to your gut feelings.

# Values and standards: What is desirable and what isn't?

Imagine the dog world was turned upside down. You would wait in anticipation for your dog to bark at another dog and immediately reward him with food when he did so. Gradually, your dog would get better and better at displaying his aggression and you would proudly show it off in front of other dog owners. On the other hand, it would be painfully embarrassing if he did a "sit". You try to prevent every attempt by your dog to sit down. In the meantime, other dog owners in the street look askance at you because he has sat down again and you start to think about looking for a dog training school. This description probably sounds very strange to

He performs a "sit" but his aggressive behaviour remains unchanged. What has been achieved?

your ears, because people would usually like to have things the other way around.

But who actually decides what dogs should and shouldn't do? We do, so we take full responsibility for it. We decide for ourselves, for society and for our dogs. All three of these parties have needs that often contradict each other and we need to find a consensus that is acceptable for everybody. The worlds in which people and dogs live are very different. Training should help everybody to become integrated into the society in which they live. That also means that we could question traditional training ideas in this respect. Did you consciously decide to teach your dog "sit"? Or did you do it because everybody does? Wouldn't your time be better spent training recall? What is your problem at the moment? That he won't sit or that he doesn't come when you call him?

The difference between conditioning and training is a whole other topic and goes beyond the scope of discussion at this point, so let's stick with "sit". Who actually decided that this action, which is very simple from an anatomical point of view, is worthy of praise? Somebody or other developed it ages ago. I can't say who was the first to do it, but it is documented as far back as the First World War and was used to create uniformity in service dog training. Sit, down, heel! In theory, it also could have included "roll over" and "paw please".

It is wonderful to imagine people in a fenced-in area shouting the command "Paw please" to their German Shepherds and it still being considered to be trivial. Believe me, it could easily have been that way! What a shame...

It goes without saying that there is nothing wrong with teaching your dog "sit". You just mustn't believe that he is trained because he does it. Please make sure that the goals for training your dog are really your own goals and whether the training content is really useful for you, your dog or society. You don't have to go along with any old rubbish, and this realisation can be very liberating.

# Learning behaviour and
# benefits
# in training

"Learning lives off the hope or fear that it could happen again."

Dogs' learning behaviour is very complex. They learn latently, motorically, through imitation and through experience. In the following, I will exclusively be concerned with the sphere of experience-related learning. It is the form of learning that is used most frequently for behavioural problems and most commonly discussed in the dog world. The focus will be on examination of suitability for work on lead aggression and no attempt will be made to explain how dogs learn in other situations.

# Classic conditioning

If a powerful blast of air comes into contact with the retina of your open eye, your eyelid will close, without you even having to think about it. Like most reflexes, the purpose of the corneal reflex is to protect the body. To speed up the reaction so that it protects the body as well as is possible, the reflex does not take the long, bureaucratic path via the brain, but is controlled directly from the spinal cord. Of course, the authority, the brain, is informed about it and a file is subsequently set up. However, the spinal cord is responsible in the first instance. Protecting the body against danger is a stressful job and working together is not always easy, but when you have been doing it for a few years, routine comes into the equation. You learn from your mistakes and simply notice the last stimulus that was there before the danger arose. For example, if you step on a shard of glass, the spinal cord attempts to prevent the worst by lifting the foot and the brain then reaches for the mobile phone to call an ambulance. In the moments before there was something that lay glittering on the ground and this was immediately noted in the file. The reflex is actually only triggered when the foot treads on the glass, but in a sensible learning process, the sight of the glittering shard will become the premonitory stimulus and will raise the foot out of the danger zone by triggering the reflex in good time. This learning process has already saved many a foot and is called classic conditioning.

## Counter conditioning

Counter conditioning is actually a good idea, but this type of conditioning is not always useful, because reactions are sometimes associated with stimuli that nobody needs. You could trigger my corneal reflex with an air pump, for example, by blowing a puff of air onto my eye. My eyelid will close, which is not conditioning or any kind of clever trick. However, if you started to whistle once just before using the air pump, a conditioning process would begin. If the whistle-air pump combination was repeated often enough, the whistle alone would be enough to close my eye by the end of the conditioning. This can be funny, but for whom? It is definitely not funny when unpleasant feelings such as anxiety or disgust are associated with certain stimuli. If something terrible happens to you in the dark, you may associate the fear reaction that has been triggered with darkness. You then experience this anxiety and try to get away as soon as darkness comes, even though nothing terrible will happen this time.

*In counter conditioning, a learned stimulus is linked with a new reaction.*

will diminish and then completely disappear. However, counter conditioning also works the other way round, for example, our mouth starts to water if we walk past a takeaway when we are hungry and smell the food. There is a good chance that we will stop and order something. If someone gave us an emetic to induce vomiting straight after we had smelt the odour and it worked immediately, the takeaway smell could gradually induce nausea and flight. This counter conditioning process is called aversion therapy. Some fast food restaurants offer aversion therapy on their menu, but in this context they also refer to it as "food".

## Counter conditioning in relation to aggression on the lead

So much for the theory, but to what extent is this knowledge useful for, or rather against, aggression on the lead? The answer depends on the dog's motives and on what he has learned previously. Counter conditioning makes sense if his aggressive behaviour was learned through classic conditioning. However, if the behaviour is down to factors other than this kind of learning process, it becomes difficult.

One of the best known counter conditioning processes is systematic desensitisation.

## Systematic desensitisation

Counter conditioning is for cases such as this. We use counter conditioning to try to erase a classic conditioned reaction. How do we do that? The old, learned stimulus is paired with a new, contradictory stimulus, which may trigger a new reaction. So, you whistle again and instead of a puff of air, you give me chocolate. If I am reliably given chocolate instead of a puff of air, the corneal reaction

Yesterday, our midwife told me a story that makes the principle of learning through classic conditioning wonderfully clear. She told me that she led a baby swimming course a few years ago. At that time, her own daughter was a baby and she took her along too. In order to show what you should do if your baby has swallowed water, she lifted her daughter up above her head with her arms outstretched. This is actually supposed to help the child get rid of the water they have swallowed, because the new position is supposed to let the water flow out of the throat through the mouth. However, the baby slipped out of her hands and fell headfirst into the water from a height of one metre, sinking beneath the surface before being pulled out of the water by her mother. The little one got a huge shock.

Until this time, our midwife's daughter had not had any problems with water. However, the bad experience led to the child becoming anxious as soon as she saw a pool of water, i.e. she associated the pool of water with the frightening situation. Or, to put it another way, the pool became a premonitory stimulus for sinking under water.

This anxiety was not just related to the swimming pool where the accident happened, but generalised to relate to anything that contained water. Even attempts to put her in a paddling pool or bathtub had to be abandoned because the baby screamed and expressed her anxiety about it. In the following weeks she could only be showered. The mother decided on systematic desensitisation to enable her child to deal with pools of water again without fear.

She put her daughter in the bathtub with toys instead of water and played with her there. Once the child was relaxed, she integrated the running tap into the game. She gradually closed the plug and the bath filled slowly while she played with her daughter. She repeated this process several times and her child's fear disappeared.

Systematic desensitisation is a behavioural therapy method that leads to elimination of fear by approaching the object step-by-step. The principle of behavioural therapy is that everything that has been learned can be un-learned again. In this case study, the desensitisation method was so successful because the child was clearly afraid and this fear had been learned.

## Therapy for anxiety

For a few years now, people on the dog scene have been doing more and more work with desensitisation. Initially, use was restricted to treatment of anxious behaviour. From the point of view of behavioural therapy, this makes sense if the anxiety reaction has been learned through classic conditioning. This does not usually include fear of shots and loud bangs, because most dogs are genuinely afraid of them and this fear does not involve a learned association. After all, counter conditioning does not make any sense for torture or rape either, because the act of violence is still there at the end. The aim is to get rid of fears and expectations that something bad could happen and, correspondingly, they may also no longer occur.

However, let's assume that the fear has been classically learned and we want to counter condition. An instant new connection is usually not possible, because the anxiety reaction is too powerful. Therefore, we approach the object of fear from a distance until the point where the dog perceives the stimulus, but does not show any anxiety and then give him food at this point, so that we are approaching stimulus that triggers fear, step-by-step. As soon as the dog reacts with anxiety that is

*Distance from the stimulus that triggers the anxiety is initially required to condition against an anxiety reaction.*

*Reduce the distance gradually and it will become possible to approach without fear.*

stronger than his pleasure about the food during the approach, take a step back until the point where he will eat again, because, as long as he can eat, he is not afraid. In order to use desensitisation to condition against a powerful emotional reaction such as fear, it is important that the fear reaction is avoided to give the new reaction more room. To begin with, this is only possible at a distance; otherwise the anxiety reaction would predominate. The stimulus that triggers anxiety diminishes with distance, so the food can be used as a new stimulus. Gradually, happiness about food will supersede the anxiety and the dog will be able eat without fear. This work is protracted and the stimulus that triggers the anxiety may only appear under controlled therapeutic conditions. Systematic desensitisation will not make any sense if the dog constantly meets this stimulus in "real life" and cannot avoid it. There are other processes in anxiety therapy for this purpose.

## When fear is not the motive

Fear is only one factor for aggression. Remember, fear flees, avoids and rarely antagonises noisily at the end of the lead. The step-by-step approach using food is now increasingly being used for aggressive behaviour that is not caused by anxiety, which is when it becomes critical, to say the least, from a professional point of view. Most motives for aggression involve the dog's desire to approach the other dog, which is why he pulls on the lead in the direction of it. These dogs do not have a problem with or fear of moving closer to the other dog. What would be the advantage of approaching step-by-step? Do you really believe that a child would behave differently at

McDonalds if you approached it with him step-by-step over a period of weeks, giving him one chip at a time? As usual, it would end with a "Happy Meal" order, but it would just take longer to get there.

Systematic desensitisation is a counter conditioning process that is used for anxiety. Correspondingly, the diagnosis for aggression on the lead must really be anxiety, so that the method actually achieves something, rather than just taking a long time.

If you have been reading attentively, you might ask at this point why aversion therapy is not used for lead aggression. The answer is simple – after all, you don't want to teach the dog that he will experience something unpleasant every time a dog appears, no matter how he behaves. That would be classic conditioning. You want to teach him that he should not act aggressively and that he is at an advantage because of the new behaviour. For this to happen, his behaviour, not the entire encounter with the dog, must lead to new consequences. This process is called operant conditioning.

## Operant conditioning

Dogs learn in a similar way to us humans. We all strive to increase our wellbeing and avoid pain and discomfort. If a given behaviour has unpleasant consequences for us, we will show it less frequently in future. However, if the behaviour has a pleasant effect, we will show it more frequently. We remember the behaviour that was successful for our respective objectives and do not make use of behaviour that will result in failure. That is the law of effect and the principle of operant or instrumental conditioning.

Remembering the places where you had previously found food or were attacked by an enemy increases chances of survival. In the first case, you will look for the place again, because the behaviour was reinforced. In the second case, you will avoid the place in future, because the behaviour was punished. Learning happens in both cases.

## Dogs wouldn't worry about pensions

Dogs live in the here and now. They can only associate both reward and punishment with their behaviour if the reward or punishment directly follows the behaviour shown. This phenomenon can even be observed in children in a rudimentary form. Sentences like "Just wait until your father gets home" or "If you're good now, we'll go to the cinema tonight" are effective, but the intensity is much less than if the consequence directly followed the behaviour.

The window of time is even smaller for dogs. Promises or threats for "later" don't produce any effect at all. Science claims that for dogs, the stimulus must follow the behaviour within 3 seconds at the most for the animal to be able to make the connection between the two.

Adult humans are much better at assessing the consequences of their behaviour. For example, they can make sacrifices to save money for something that will happen in the future. A dog, on the other hand, would spend the money straight away because he can't think that far ahead into the future and does

Dogs *live in the here and now.*
*They have no interest in promises*
*or threats for the future.*

not see any benefit to making sacrifices in the short term. As I write this, it strikes me that I am probably more like a dog.

You could say that people are experts in the future and that dogs are experts in the present. Both learn from the past. People plan, think, ponder over things, imagine the future and develop strategies for it. Dogs do not postpone anything, but act and see what consequences result for them.

## How can I get you to take a headache tablet?

I could suggest a deal such as every time you take a tablet, I'll give you 30,000 euros. Interested? Please don't ask me about the side effects. A dog wouldn't and I'm trying to create a plausible example after all. So, let's assume that it gives you a boost and that you will take one tablet after the other if you have any money worries in the future. This kind of action is called positive reinforcement because something pleasant is being added.

However, I could also wait until you are suffering with a headache. If I give you a tablet then and you discover that it soothes your pain, you will remember this for the future and reach for the tablets as soon as you feel a headache coming on. This is called negative reinforcement, because something unpleasant, in this case a headache, is taken away.

In both cases, the behaviour "taking tablets" will be reinforced and shown more frequently in the future. With positive reinforcement, the offer of money is tempting and with negative reinforcement, the chance to end suffering is attractive.

## How can I get you to stop driving too fast?

You are in a hurry and step on the accelerator to get to where you need to be faster. Your behaviour is putting you and others in danger, but, unfortunately, you are not aware of this. That is why the Road Traffic Act and penalties exist. If I want to spoil driving too fast for you, in order to protect you and others from yourself, I also have two options as follows.

I could wave you over to the side, spit on a handkerchief and use it to meticulously clean the corners of your mouth. You would then be allowed to drive away immediately. I am adding something unpleasant and you are able to associate it with what you did wrong. This is called positive punishment.

However, I could also pull you over and take away your car key for an hour, preventing you from driving on for this long period. As a result, I would be taking away the appeal of speeding, namely, that of saving time. Punishment that involves taking away something pleasant is called negative punishment.

In both cases, driving too fast will be punished and shown less frequently in the future. With positive punishment, the expectation of somebody else's bodily fluid on your face will prevent you from driving too fast again in the future. With negative punishment, on the other hand, it is the loss of time-saving.

## "Positive" and "negative" do not mean "good" and "evil".

As the example shows, there are two types of reinforcement and two types of punishment. The difference is marked by the words "positive" and "negative". In this context, "positive" means that a stimulus follows a particular behaviour; "negative", on the other hand, means that a stimulus is removed, taken away or otherwise avoided when certain behaviour is shown. The result is positive and negative reinforcement and positive and negative punishment.

|  | Behaviour shown more often | Behaviour shown less often |
|---|---|---|
| Stimulus is added or presented | Positive reinforcement (something pleasant is added) | Positive punishment (something unpleasant is added) |
| Stimulus is taken away or not presented | Negative reinforcement (something unpleasant is taken away) | Negative punishment (something pleasant is taken away) |

## Positive reinforcement – a behaviour should be shown more often

Let's begin with the pleasant side of learning, i.e. encouragement and motivation. When the dog does something we like, we reward him by giving him something for it. This can be verbal praise, a pat, food, a favourite toy or even just a smile and a glance. Something pleasant is added. In this case, the dog's tastes will determine what is pleasant. But how does this knowledge help me when it comes to the problem on the lead?

## Positive reinforcement in relation to aggression on the lead

On the one hand, positive reinforcement can explain how people may have subconsciously reinforced the unwanted behaviour. If the owner looks at his dog during the conflict, speaks to him (whether in a calming or antagonising tone) and gives the dog his attention as a result, then he is rewarding the dog for his aggressive behaviour. You could say that every unsuccessful thing you do in the heat of the conflict further reinforces the dog's unwanted behaviour.

# Positive reinforcement in relation to conflict resolution

On the other hand, the use of positive reinforcement can also represent a solution. For example, the dog could be taught to look at his owner and this visual contact could be rewarded with food if he is not engaged in a conflict. Initially, every look is acknowledged and then the dog will have to look for longer each time. Only when he can show the new behaviour over a longer period do we do it under signal control and add a name to the action, for example, "watch". In the next step, we practise the new behaviour in conflict. The dog is led to another dog and given the signal "watch". If he shows this behaviour and walks past the other dog while looking at his owner, he is praised when the situation comes to an end. When you begin this work, the dog should always be rewarded, but when the dog consistently shows the new behaviour, it should be only acknowledged every now and then. In positive reinforcement, you are bringing the behaviour patterns – "aggression" and "watch" – into competition with one another.

With this method, it is up to the dog to decide which behaviour to show. The owner offers the dog a new way to behave. If the dog accepts this offer, he does it gladly and of his own free will, which is enormously beneficial to his learning.

However, if he does not accept it, this method does not give the owner any other options for influencing the dog's behaviour, because the dog does not learn that he may not act aggressively; he just learns to show a different behaviour. If the aggression is limited to the lead alone and the dog reliably accepts the alternative behaviour that he has been trained to perform, then learning through positive behaviour is possible in a relaxed setting.

# Limitations and disadvantages of positive reinforcement

As we have already mentioned, the disadvantage of using positive reinforcement to work with lead aggression is that the dog does not become inhibited in showing aggressive behaviour but just learns to display a different behaviour instead, which is then rewarded. If the dog also causes problems with other dogs when running free, working on the lead using reward would not make any sense. This kind of training cannot be maintained when off the lead, i.e. in direct contact with others.

## Distraction: a way out of the dilemma?

So there I am. I have been practising "watch" with no distractions for weeks and now I feel ready. The other dog is coming and my dog and I notice him. When I say "watch", my dog briefly looks up at me and then at the other dog. He has decided against the alternative behaviour and lunges at the end of the lead, barking. How am I supposed to reward behaviour when the dog doesn't show it? The solution is called distraction. That means that you do not ask the dog for an

*With distraction, the reinforcer is always there.*

*Unlike counter conditioning, the dog is only given the food when he has shown the correct behaviour.*

alternative behaviour that has been trained in advance and then acknowledge it at the end, but try to focus the dog on the reward before the conflict and guide him through the situation with the promise of the reward. This increases the chances of the dog staying calm. Because of the constant presence of the reward, the dog has the option of concentrating on it. Unlike reinforcement of alternative behaviour, the reward must always be present in this method. The dog does not learn any new behaviour patterns but just looks at the object of distraction. If the distraction isn't there, he will fall back into his old behaviour patterns. Therefore, it is important to gradually begin only rewarding the desired behaviour and reducing the initial distraction. However, when working with a distraction, the dog may choose aggression instead of food. Work with a distraction is often confused with counter conditioning. In the latter, the dog gets the food as soon as he has noticed the other dog. With distraction, he gets the reward when he behaves correctly.

The term "deflection" should be differentiated from distraction. With deflection, the dog may continue to behave aggressively, but his behaviour is deflected to a different object. For example, letting him bite into a bite tug toy allows him to get rid of his aggression. How much is achieved by this is definitely questionable, but deflection must be mentioned at this point as a further method.

## Incorrect timing

Incorrect timing and the build-up of chain reactions that it facilitates is a problem both in reinforcement and in punishment patterns. In punishment, it also explains the phenomenon of masochism, but more about that later. A mistake in the structure of the work can lead to the opposite of the learning goal in positive reinforcement too.

For example, if you often call your dog back to you when he runs away and then reward him with food when he comes back, you will notice something. From a subjective point of view, the owner is training the dog's recall, but the dog is learning something quite different at the same time. If he is interested in the reward, the dog will wonder how he can get it. The learning result will be that the dog frequently runs away. Strange? – no, not at all. Because he has learned that he has to run away in order to be called back and given the associated food reward. We call this an event chain. It would actually be more sensible to give a dog food when he stays with you and not to give him any when he runs away. If you

want to use food to work on lead aggression, it is important to make sure that the dog is

*In deflection, behaviour does not change, it is just deflected onto a different object.*

quiet throughout the entire encounter and that only this is rewarded. If you begin to acknowledge the dog every time he looks at you during a conflict (shaping), even though he is aggressive in between times, the consequence may be that an event chain is learned: bark, look, food. As a result the problem will still be there and will become more firmly established. This is a serious error, especially in distraction.

## Food for the culprit

Imagine two mothers meeting, each holding their four-year-old son by the hand. One calls from a distance "Is that a boy?" The other is clearly uptight as she nods in reply to the question. Now they both take a packet of sweets out of their pocket, hold them in front of their sons' faces and lead the boys past each other. Then they each take a few sweets out of the bag and give them to their sons, saying "Thank you. It was so nice of you not to be aggressive." Do you find that strange? Nowadays, that is completely normal for dogs. The crazy thing is that only dogs that have behaved aggressively at some point get food when they meet other dogs. Dogs that have always been relaxed on the lead do not get anything. Unfortunately, dogs don't just learn what people would like them to learn. Along with being rewarded for the correct behaviour pattern, the dog takes on the entire learning situation at the same time, which means that the reward raises the value of encountering other dogs. The aim should actually be to give dogs the chance to experience meeting other dogs as something normal and trivial, but that can be difficult when every encounter on the lead becomes a highlight. Why should a dog stop barking when it seems to be so important?

## Everybody has their own truth

We people like to believe that, when it comes to dogs, we are the only ones that reinforce their behaviour and that we just have to get it right. That means that we reward the dog when he sits and waits quietly and do not give him anything when he is pushy and demanding. Many of dogs' learning experiences have little to do with people's reactions as reinforcement. When it comes to aggression on the lead, the dog's owner, the other dog, bystanders, food, a ball, as well as a release of hormones, can all act as a reward. Anything that is important to the dog reinforces him. Aggression makes others want to get involved and it can be definitely be self-rewarding. For example, if the aggressive behaviour is socially reinforced, it is difficult to go into successful competition with this reinforcer using food. The reward must always come first in the dog's personal ranking, otherwise positive reinforcement will only work at a distance, i.e. far away from conflict.

## The most important thing is to look good – social reinforcers

It is the beginning of January 2011 and we northern Germans no longer have to bring up the snow catastrophe of 1976/77 to explain to the rest of the Republic that we know what winter is too. We are already into our second year of winter. In the state of Schleswig-Holstein that doesn't just mean snow, ice and temperatures of minus ten, but wind too. And the wind is like a knife. But we have adapted to it and we are well equipped in the clothes department. Admittedly, our efforts are still a little clumsy and we are definitely not as chic as the people in Kitzbühel, but practicality is the main thing. Out in the country, trends catch on a little late, even among our young people. While boys in the centre of Berlin are letting their hair grow long again, the gelled, short hairstyle is still en vogue round our

way. And this, superficial aspects aside, is also a learning theory phenomenon.

They wait at the bus stop at 7.15 am, dressed to impress. They are male and aged between 14 and 16 years. The wind is whistling, the snow is blowing in sideways and they have gel on their hair and no hats. The crazy thing is that they know how a hat works. They would have had hats put on them in early childhood, i.e. during their sensitive phase. They would have been very well used to hats

*Even impressing another dog is a success that can become a reinforcer.*

and have experienced the benefits of this piece of clothing. They also know about the pain of cold because they suffer it every day. But they defy it, along with their parents' annoyance, and remain hatless.

This phenomenon is called social self-presentation or, to put it another way, true heroes are not just brave but also a little stupid. Presenting themselves to each other and, most importantly, to the opposite sex is more important than not freezing and it is reinforced by social mechanisms. This aspect is often underestimated in dog training. Making an impression to present yourself to the outside world is an important part of sexual behaviour. Or do you really think that high heels are comfortable to wear?

Why, however, communities in Northern Germany ran out of grit after just a week of snow is not as easy to explain and has nothing at all to do with learning theory. Oh well, Pavlov and Skinner didn't come from Schleswig-Holstein after all.

## Are dogs actually football fans?

Dogs will get into several combative altercations in their lives whether we want them to or not. There will be conflicts whenever we allow our dogs to interact with other members of their species. As we have already mentioned, disharmony is part of social cooperation. A conflict that takes place openly involves a decision and usually ends with victory or defeat.

*If you know that somebody is holding onto you, you can lean far out of the window.*

*Along with the owner's judgement, hormones can also reinforce behaviour.*

One exception is the situation on the lead. When on their leads, dogs can behave aggressively without having to get into a direct conflict. We humans are happy to help by holding on tightly to both rivals and leading them safely past one another. This makes it easy for dogs to antagonise and stare at each other from a distance when they pass and then mutually take flight. It's a veritable win-win situation! Both dogs feel that they have won. The goal of increasing the distance has been achieved and acts as a reinforcer for behaviour.

But what happens hormonally when we win or lose? A study of male football fans got to the bottom of this question. The testosterone levels of fans of both teams were measured before the game and then again after the game for comparison. The result was that the testosterone levels of the fans of the winning team had risen. The testosterone levels of the fans of the losing team had fallen. Testosterone makes you self-confident and increases your willingness to take risks. The chances of winning again in the next fight increase with the testosterone level.

Congratulations, you've got a real winner on the end of your lead. But why aren't you happy about it? Many dog owners feel that their walk is a daily battle, so they try to stop their dog's aggressive tendencies. If this doesn't work, it has totally different consequences for people and dogs. The dog feels like the winner in the conflict with the other

*Both dogs leave this situation as winners. The owners, on the other hand, feel like losers.*

dog and the owner feels like the loser in the conflict with their own dog. The more often you are defeated, the more difficult a victory becomes.

On the one hand, failure causes the owner's expectation that the dog will be aggressive when it encounters another dog to increase. It is a kind of self-fulfilling prophecy that directs perception and body language to the problem, making conditions favourable for aggressive behaviour as a result. On the other hand, losing also has a hormonal effect. Stress, shown by cortisol levels, increases and testosterone levels decrease. Repeated "losing" is pre-programmed.

The owner's desire to avoid further meetings with dogs is understandable because of the association with negative feelings. Unfortunately, from a dog's point of view, we do not necessarily appear to be socially competent during attempts to flee. Dogs' perception of body language and chemical communication in people is finely tuned. They will take note of the change and attach a higher value to the entire situation. Furthermore, aggressive behaviour is self-rewarding from a hormonal point of view.

## Does success really make you rich and sexy?

Joe Herbert and John Coates found out how influential the sex hormone testosterone is in their study of stockbrokers. A high concentration of testosterone in the blood makes stockbrokers more successful. Stockbrokers who have a very high testosterone level early in the morning will probably have a successful working day. This can probably be attributed to the fact that a high testosterone level makes you confident and increases your willingness to take risks. Under some circumstances, this has a positive effect on the stockbrokers' daily statement.

However, constant winning also has its dangers. Both scientists established that the winning feeling among successful stockbrokers led in turn to more testosterone being released, which can ultimately lead to hubris, with risky consequences. "If testosterone levels become excessive, as may be the case in economic bubbles, the desire for risk may become excessive." For some reason, many a male terrier now springs to mind.

## Thanks, I'm full!

The dog decides what is perceived to be a reward. But it isn't just about his preferences; it is also partly related to standard of living. The more somebody has, the more it takes to make them happy. It sounds terrible, but the greater the need, the higher the motivation. What would you do for ⇔1,000? Probably more than a multimillionaire would. It's similar with dogs. Because our dogs have their needs in many areas so well taken care of, we have to go to extremes. If we talk to them lovingly all day long, stroke and massage them for hours, feed them only the best and allow them constant access to toys, there is really very little left to give. So, if you have to go on bended knee before your dog, appealing to him in a high-pitched voice and plying him with sausages for him to show the faintest glimmer of happiness and he then just irritably pulls his head away when you want to stroke him, then you could start to worry about this issue. But, then again, maybe you have a Labrador for whom every day is a new adventure.

## Eat or die!

The power of positive reinforcement increases in proportion to the need for something, so if a dog were really hungry, he would be more willing to show the desired behaviour. Correct. Social starvation works in a similar way. However, aggression on the lead is important for some dogs for reasons we have already covered and they cannot be dissuaded from it as easily. How unpleasant do we have to make things for the dog so that we can use positive reinforcement? Is it fair to deprive the dog of all attention and food for most of the day so that you can use these things as rewards when he meets another dog? Do you have to starve your dog for the method to work? There are studies in this area that represent a form of mental cruelty through social coldness in their extremity and abuse: "I only love you when you are good!"

## Negative reinforcement – a behaviour should be shown more often

Behaviour can be reinforced, not just by giving something pleasant, but by taking away something unpleasant. If a puppy has fallen asleep away from his siblings and wakes up cold and lonely, he will seek the closeness of his littermates, lie with them and warm up. The next time he is cold or feels alone, he will cuddle up with his siblings again. The elimi-

nation of cold and social isolation acts as the reinforcer. How can this knowledge help me when it comes to problems on the lead?

## Negative reinforcement in relation to the problem

Negative reinforcement can explain, for example, why some insecure and, above all, anxious dogs learn aggressive behaviour. The direct proximity of other dogs makes them uneasy. By quickly dashing forward and then pulling back again, they keep the other dog at a distance and their discomfort disappears. Frustrated dogs also learn in a similar way. They are in an unpleasant state of excitement because of their frustration. Their aggressive behaviour enables them to give vent to their anger and find their way back to a normal physiological state.

## Negative reinforcement in relation to conflict resolution

In dog training, lead aggression is now rarely dealt with using negative reinforcement. The method, which namely involved putting the dog in a continuously unpleasant situation first, to then be able to take away the unpleasantness, used to be used frequently. A typical example of this is "hanging" the dog. If a dog was aggressive, he was pulled up on a short lead until he was standing on just two legs and then held there. He was only allowed to stand on all four legs and breathe again when he showed the desired behaviour. In order for this method to work, you would have to leave what I consider to be the ethically justifiable area of dog training and it therefore cannot constitute a training tip.

However, you could apply a milder version of this principle. Tie your dog to a post and stand a few metres away from it. The dog must find this distance to be unpleasant. Now send for another dog and position it opposite your dog. If your own dog is quiet, reduce the unpleasant distance by approaching him. If he starts to bark again, back off. (However, this would be negative punishment.) When he is friendly again, remove the unpleasant situation.

*Aggression keeps other dogs at a distance and can be learned as a strategy.*

# Limitations and disadvantages of negative reinforcement

Not everything that works is allowed. Not everything that is allowed works. It goes without saying that these two sentences apply to all four types of operant conditioning. However, they become very clear in negative reinforcement. The dog would have to be put in a very unpleasant situation for negative reinforcement to work properly and not take ages. This is not acceptable to human beings for emotional reasons. When you look at the second description, you wonder how long it would take and whether you would always be able to find a tree or post at the right time. A negative punishment has already been included in this example. In its milder form, negative reinforcement works well and we will see it again later, but it would be very difficult to create a meaningful learning situation using negative reinforcement alone. The fundamental difficulty of using reinforcement in cases of failure is the same for positive and negative reinforcement. After all, their purpose in learning is to make behaviour appear more often.

# Positive punishment – a behaviour should be shown less often

Now we come to the methods where the aim is for behaviours to be shown less frequent-ly. The purpose of positive punishment is to teach how to inhibit behaviour and it often concerns inhibiting end actions. Learning bite inhibition is a good example of this. Two puppies play together, biting each other as they do so. When one of the puppies bites too hard, the other will defend itself by biting back equally hard. The first puppy will learn that biting too hard had unpleasant consequences for him and will play more "gently" in future. However, he will not develop a fear of playing or of other dogs because of this learning process. The relaxed fighting game may even continue after the brief altercation or it may be continued later. The punishment was only about biting too hard and inhibits this behaviour as a result. If, on the other hand, a puppy was attacked several times by other dogs as soon as the puppy met them on a walk and his behaviour was not relevant to these attacks, it could lead to a learned aversion. The appearance of other dogs would become a trigger for the fear that he will be bitten again. The difference is not in the type of punishment but in the timing.

# Positive punishment in relation to aggression on the lead

Knowledge about punishment cannot be used to explain how dogs learn aggressive behaviour on the lead, because behaviour that is punished will occur more seldom in the future. However, it does explain very well how people learn to avoid meeting other dogs while theirs is on the lead. In positive punishment, something unpleasant is added and that is exactly what happens to people with a lead-aggressive dog. The unpleasant stimulus may be pain in the shoulder that is experienced when the dog furiously leaps to the end of his lead. It may also be shock, panic or insults from other dog owners. If you find something like that to be unpleasant, it can result in you trying less and less often to walk past other dogs.

# Positive punishment in relation to conflict resolution

When positive punishment is used in lead aggression, it is supposed to inhibit the dog's aggressive behaviour. That does not mean that the entire encounter with another dog should have unpleasant consequences for your dog, just the aggressive behaviour. When working with positive punishment, it is important to make sure that only the aggressive behaviour is punished and that the dog is given the chance to choose an alternative behaviour that could replace the old behaviour when the exercise is repeated.

It actually sounds quiet simple: when the dog starts to behave aggressively on the lead, the behaviour is punished and will be shown less frequently by the dog in future. However, it is not that easy, because punishments do not come running to the rescue, they have to be carried out by somebody and that is the problem. Everything would be wonderful if all you needed to do was skilfully say "no" at the right time. Unfortunately, dogs do not have

a built-in "no" gene. For many, the spoken word is little more than hot air to begin with. That means that, in this method, the person has to do something that the dog finds unpleasant. The dog will determine what he finds unpleasant. Strategies in this area are certainly the subject of arguments. Methods that cause the dog fear and pain are to be refused on ethical grounds, but even if a punishment is not associated with fear and pain, it will affect the dog and may also make him insecure to begin with. It is then important to give the dog confidence again and help him to connect to the person and show a different type of behaviour. With positive punishment, unlike positive reinforcement, the dog does not decide whether to participate. He does not abandon his aggressive behaviour voluntarily, but because he has to. There are advantages and disadvantages to this fact. Misuse of power is the greatest danger and there are studies in this field whose extremity leads to a form of physical and emotional abuse of dogs.

# Punishment now has a new look

Nowadays, people don't like to use words like punishment, which are associated with violence and unfairness. We prefer to talk about consequences, setting boundaries or interrupting unwanted behaviour. In terms of the psychology of learning, it does not make a difference, but it does emotionally. The new terms are supposed to express empathy, appropriateness and goodwill, which is why they are important. Positive punishment must not end with oppression of or violence against the dog or be seen as carte blanche for this kind of behaviour. Setting boundaries can strengthen a trusting relationship, because it gives the dog a framework within which he can act safety and securely. However, a dog needs to learn how to deal with conflict. Social friction and quarrelling can even be fun if they lead to clarity and greater closeness to the dog. However, punishment can also damage a relationship if it is an act of revenge without prior clarification of the relationship, if it is emotionally charged, badly timed, happens without giving any alternatives and if no thought is given to appropriateness. People who take pleasure in punishing shouldn't have dogs.

# Limitations and disadvantages of positive punishment

The question of motives is important in positive punishment too. For example, punishment may be more than counterproductive in anxious and traumatised dogs. Try punishing the behaviour of a drowning man who is fighting for his life and thrashing about, so that you can rescue him more easily. It wouldn't work. All you can do is hold him and somehow get him onto land.

## Sometimes I'm not allowed – always punish?

The most effective and sustainable method for reducing the frequency of a behaviour is to punish any unwanted reactions, but it is rarely enough to only punish the reactions every now and then. For dogs that only yap along in response to another dog, infrequent interruptions may reduce occurrences of the behaviour. However, aggressive behaviour is usually purposeful, useful and often involves self-rewarding patterns. From a human point of view, we punish every now and then and from a canine point of view behaviour is reinforced every now and then, so it is worth the dog's while to keep trying the behaviour as long as there is hope that it might work this time. This means that, for a certain time, the owner will have to be very attentive in monitoring their dog. Your own emotional ups and downs may impede the work here and, to put it plainly, this can be a disadvantage and rather stressful when it comes to working with positive punishment.

## Behavioural motivation and intensity

The efficacy of a punishment depends on the dog's motivations, among other factors. If a dog is very highly motivated to show behaviour, he will tolerate a certain amount of punishment and will only allow himself to be interrupted if the punishment is high intensity.

A good example of this is hunting behaviour. If a dog is highly motivated to hunt, for example, because of his genetic disposition, then it will be very difficult to control this behaviour. In order to respond appropriately to aggressive behaviour on the lead, it is important to clarify the dog's motives and how high his motivation is.

## 1

Lead aggression is an insidious process and often starts with harmless yapping.

By the time the owner becomes fully aware of the problem, the intensity of the behaviour is usually already very high.

*These two male dogs are serious. It is understandable that dog owners try to avoid encounters like this. However, flight seldom helps to resolve the conflict.*

*The intensity of the behaviour should be an important factor in choosing a method. Dogs would need good reason to still be aware of and influenced by their owners in this situation.*

## Punishment and reluctance

Some dog owners happily report that their dog has stopped chasing horses because he had a chance encounter with the paddock fence. Some owners wish that their dog would just come across the "right" person when off their lead who would put them in their place. On the one hand, statements such as these describe the blatant hope that the dog will associate his unwanted behaviour with an unpleasant experience. On the other hand, it also reveals that the owners would like the effect to be remote and do not want to be involved themselves. It may sound strange at first, but this phenomenon is not unusual and it can be found in many areas of society. People often only use punishment reluctantly. Sociologist Niklas Luhmann wrote: "Communication is a constant risk." People are afraid of being rejected by their social counterparts if they set clear boundaries and there is a great fear that if you stop a dog from doing something he will stop loving you or even pack his little case and move out. If this fear is not expressed and people are compelled by external forces to punish their dogs, then it can lead to the cycle of anger and guilt that has already been described. Humans are marked out by their unwillingness to punish and, when I look at a lot of work in the sphere of interrupting behaviour, the worry that lies behind this unwillingness is justified. If dogs only learn that they get into trouble when they do something that we consider to be wrong and if they do not get the chance to avoid being in trouble by showing alternative behaviour, they admittedly won't move out, but they will also never be confident and secure.

## Availability of alternative behaviour patterns

"What use is it for me to know what's wrong, if I don't know what's right?"

For a punishment to be effective in the long term and also for it to be fair to the dog, it is important that the dog is able to choose an alternative behaviour. This sounds simple. Many dog trainers suggest commands such as "sit" or "down" as alternative behaviours, which is a good idea, but often does not get to the heart of the issue. Some dogs are more than capable of continuing to behave aggressively from a sitting or lying position. These alternative behaviours calm the dog down physically but his voice remains the same. It is obviously easier to give commands than to change the dog's mood, because this would involve the owner exerting a powerful social influence, which is something that most owners do not do. It also does not have anything to do with psychology of learning, so we will look at it in more detail in the following chapters. So, returning to learning behaviour: if possible, the alternative behaviour should be incompatible with the unwanted behaviour.

Work with three different dogs is shown on the DVD of the same name that accompanies this book. One of our case studies was Jeanny, a small, female Maltese Terrier. Jeanny behaved very insecurely towards other dogs and, until training began, aggressively kept all dogs away by barking and snapping. Only after her aggressive behaviour had been interrupted did she make a tentative attempt at social contact. For the first time in her life, she actually sniffed another dog. This new behaviour was an important learning experience for Jeanny and, at the same time, it constituted a genuine alternative. The friendly greeting of another dog is not compatible with aggression. In this case, it was important to allow her to greet the other dog on her lead and to bolster her in her new behaviour. This alternative behaviour could perhaps have been harmful in a different case. It would be the wrong alternative if, for example, a dog finds it difficult to endure not being allowed to get to another dog because he is on his lead and becomes aggressive when he meets dogs as a result of this. In this case, it would be more sensible to quieten down the dog and reward this behaviour before going back into the conflict. For other dogs, the alternatives may be related to their owner, for example, instead of acting aggressively, they can show friendly

*Interrupting aggressive behaviour allows dogs to develop a new behavioural idea, which should be encouraged by the owner.*

and submissive behaviour to their owners. This kind of alternative would have to be considered and developed under the heading of taking guidance from the owner when on the lead.

Searching for food or carrying objects could also be used as alternatives, even if the social aspects are unfortunately not in the foreground here. Reinforcement of alternative behaviour must not be confused with distracting the dog. In distraction, we do not stop an unwanted behaviour and then reinforce an alternative one. The aim of distraction is for the dog not to show the behaviour in the first place because of the distraction. This is also an option, but the aim is different. In this case, alternative behaviour is what is offered after punishment, because if dogs do not have any new solutions they have to keep returning to their old behaviour.

## Learning theorists are sadists

If you read about learning behaviour in scientific books and come across the theme of punishment, one sentence will always crop up: hit hard and early. Whenever I read this motto, I can immediately picture it written on a black sign hanging over the door to an S&M club. But are learning theorists really sadists? I don't know, but the sentence is the result of scientific investigations. The earlier the punishment comes and the more powerful it is, the greater the chance that the behaviour will no longer be shown. Dogs and people can get used to punishment if the intensity is increased slowly. In the end, even high intensity is no longer enough, because they have had enough time to learn to tolerate the punishment and to ignore it by intensifying

their own behaviour. In the same way, we can gradually get used to cold, heat, pain, shock or discomfort. If this basic rule is applied, it would mean that if you don't want your dog to hunt, then you should punish him at a high intensity as soon as he shows any interest in wildlife as a puppy. It actually sounds logical, but, luckily, nobody would do it. What stops us isn't science but our love for dogs and fairness towards them. We try to come up with an appropriate punishment, but what does appropriate actually mean? You could base this decision on the type of the offence. After all, it does make a difference for us whether a dog raided a rubbish bin or threatened a child. In terms of learning theory, the difference would be irrelevant, but emotionally it wouldn't. It is always difficult if the unwanted behaviour develops over time, because it can be hard to judge. Aggressive behaviour on the lead usually starts insidiously and gradually gets worse. If some people had known what would happen later, they would probably have nipped it in the bud. Along with learning theory, intensity of punishment also depends on the social structures between the owner and the dog. The more important the owner is for the dog, the less they have to do to be heard.

## Here we go – punishment as a trigger for aggression

Two adult male dogs circle each other. Their body language is imposing, their bodies ramrod stiff and their gaze locked onto each other. You could cut the atmosphere with a knife and then one of them loses his nerve: no, not one of the dogs, but one of the owners. There is a sound of whistling through the air and then the flying lead hits one of the dogs on its hip. What happens next is not what the person that hit the dog had intended. The dogs fight. The fight was triggered by hitting the dog, which was intended to act as an interruption. How did this happen? The first thing to mention here is timing: the interruption clearly came too late. The dog that was hit by the lead would have reacted with a minimal uncontrolled movement, but the tenseness of the situation did not allow this, so the other dog took it as a trigger to allow the existing conflict to escalate. Furthermore, there were also no alternative options for the dog whose behaviour was interrupted. Where was he supposed to go after the punishment? He was too close to the other dog to be able to retreat after the blow. Then there is the attention that all of the bystanders are directing at the dogs. In this case, intervention may be interpreted by the dogs as more participation. Some people say that the dog maybe thought it was the other dog and not the lead. Even

*If dogs are communicating aggressively at close range, attempts at punishment often trigger an escalation in conflict. (Photo: Nadin Matthews)*

that is theoretically possible, but I personally think that dogs are a little more intelligent than that. Similar things can be observed in aggression on the lead. The owner's attempt to nip their dog's behaviour in the bud can be a trigger for aggression, which is often related to the emotional appraisal, but also to timing and intensity.

## Masochism or the nicer side of punishment

How can you teach a dog to enjoy an effect such as being jerked by their lead? For example, you could jerk gently on the lead and reward the dog immediately with one of his favourite foods. Gradually increase the strength of the jerk following the same principle. As a result, he will learn that the jerk means food and will experience it as being pleasant, i.e. yanking the lead becomes a promise that a reward will follow immediately. You are probably wondering who would do such a silly thing. I would say almost every dog owner who has a problem with aggression on the lead. Not intentionally of course, because many are simply not aware of the learning effect. Punishment that involves a high degree of emotional participation by the owner and therefore a lot of attention may be learnt by dogs as a cue. If people then think that they have to reward or feed straight after the punishment, a completely different learning result will soon be established, in that dogs may learn to seek moments of punishment to receive reinforcement in the form of attention or food. Learning theorists see a similar explanation in some cases of masochism. Self-injurious behaviour often brings the individual reinforcement in the form of sympathy and attention. Thus, the unpleasant aspect of self-injury is learned as a cue for reinforcement.

You should avoid making a direct link between punishment and reward. It makes more sense not to reward after interrupting a dog's unwanted behaviour, but to leave the situation as it is and return to it again after a short time. If the dog behaves differently at the next attempt, without you having to influence him, then a reward is appropriate.

## Frustration spoils your chances

Some people need to be very frustrated to overcome their reluctance to interrupt their dog's behaviour. As we have already mentioned, this can result in timing problems and overreactions. However, learning specialists assert that there is another, completely different problem in that a punishment loses meaning if the person doing the punishing is perceived as being unsure and frustrated. Based on my observations of parents and their children in various DIY stores across the world, I can confirm that this is the case. Reprimanding children seems like an act of desperation and constitutes a strong emotional reaction on behalf of the parents, as well as a punishment. In turn, it raises the value of the conflict situation or is seen as hostile behaviour and is responded to accordingly, so frustration-driven setting of boundaries can contribute to escalation of a conflict that did not even exist before. Within such conflicts, the degree of new frustration increases on both sides and mutual understanding is reduced to a minimum. Frustration in turn causes aggression, both in the person and in the dog.

*When people are frustrated, they shouldn't take out their anger on the dog, because it will lead to social distance rather than learning success.*

# Negative punishment by removing a pleasant stimulus

Supernanny, who devised the concept of the "naughty step", has become known for negative punishment. In learning psychology, we call the withdrawal of closeness and attention as a consequence of unwanted behaviour the "time-out" method. For social beings, unwanted isolation from the group or the loss of attention is a punishment. For example, if a dog whimpers and barks because he wants to be petted and the owner wants to get him out of the habit of using attention-seeking behaviour, the owner could take him by the collar and shut him out of the room, without saying anything. This behaviour will become less frequent after a few repetitions. The pleasant closeness is taken away from him when he starts to whimper or bark.

# Negative punishment in relation to aggression on the lead

Negative punishment cannot explain how dogs learn aggressive behaviour either. However, people learn too and negative punishment can greatly reduce the desire to walk past another dog. When the weather isn't foul, taking the dog for a walk can do people good. Imagine walking through the neighbourhood with your dog, chatting with him, maybe playing with him, enjoying the exercise in the fresh air together or just daydreaming. The atmosphere is good, but changes rapidly as soon as another dog appears on the scene. Within seconds, the owner's mood is dominated by negative feelings. The pleasant mood created by being alone is taken away. In terms of learning theory, the result would be that the human shows the behaviour "walking past another dog" less frequently.

# Negative punishment in relation to conflict resolution

Taking away something pleasant? In order to work with this technique, it is firstly important to find out what the dog finds pleasant about the situation. In the description with the attention-seeking dog, it's easy: he wants the closeness and attention of the human. If you take one or even both of these things away from him when he barks, he may associate this with his behaviour and this is the origin of the most popular dog training technique: ignoring, i.e. the conscious withdrawal of attention. If the dog's lead aggression is actually and exclusively about attention from the owner, this technique cannot be beaten for simplicity. Take your dog for a walk on his lead and give him all the attention in the world. That means looking at him, talking to him, stroking him and maybe even giving him food. If another dog appears, you should initially stay in "caring mode". Only when your own dog is preparing for aggressive behaviour, i.e. focusing his gaze

*Walks would be wonderful
if there were no other dogs.*

*But walks could also be wonderful
if your own dog behaved differently.*

*Withdrawal of attention is a popular solution strategy. But does it work?*

on the other dog and straightening his legs etc., should you remove all the attention and demonstratively turn away from the dog. When the dog reconnects with his owner, he gets attention again. As a result, the dog may learn that his aggressive behaviour leads to withdrawal of social appraisal and he may show it more rarely in future.

# Limitations and disadvantages of negative punishment

Ignoring only helps if the dog's aggression is motivated by social attention from his owner. However, withdrawal of attention is not necessarily the solution, even in dogs who display socially-motivated aggression, because they still have something, i.e. proximity to their owner, which is an important factor for aggressive behaviour. We could enhance the technique and take proximity away from the dog by tying him to a tree or a post as a consequence and then retreating to a distance. This technique will work really well if aggression is socially motivated. However, if there are other factors for the dog, for example, defending its territory, sexual competition and so on, work using withdrawal of social proximity will reach its limitations at this point.

Furthermore, you will need somewhere to tie your dog every time you meet another dog. There is another version that does not involve a tree or similar, but involves sending the dog away on the lead. We will come to this technique shortly.

# "Right, I'm off" – flight as punishment?

For dogs that are still learning to be aggressive on the lead and haven't already been showing this behaviour for months, there is another way to work with negative punishment. For example, when the aggressive behaviour starts, you can drop the lead and walk away. Many young dogs are unsettled when their owner is no longer near and they are not heroes on their own. In all activities that are based on the person leaving the situation, you must consider what you are teaching on a social level as a result. Are you maybe abandoning an insecure dog? Are you teaching the dog that you always run away from conflicts instead of seeing them through with him?

## Inhibition in public

Simply dropping the lead and walking away or tying the dog to a tree and continuing sound easy at first, but have you ever tried leaving an angry child at the checkout and walking away? There are no longer just two people in this communication. Bystanders will want to take the opportunity to evaluate your attempts at education. You are either a bad mother if you walk away or inconsistent because you buy the lolly. There is always something …

# Appropriate combinations and feasibility

To make good use of learning theory so that dogs can learn quickly, the four types of operant conditioning can be combined in one learning situation. One example of this is sending away. I developed this technique taking into consideration learning behaviour, as well as social aspects and, above all, feasi-bility. Sending away is not a panacea and, like every other technique, it depends on the owner-dog relationship and the motives for aggression. However, it is a good way of describing how reinforcement and punishment

*The dog is sent away using body language.*

*The distance is maintained for a few seconds.*

can be combined.

**You could try the following:**

As soon as the dog fixes his gaze on another dog and starts to attack it, the owner stands in front of their own dog and simultaneously frightens it with a loud noise by hitting their thigh with their hand or the lead. This shock is a positive punishment.

Then, the owner sends away their dog, using body language and a threatening glare, by

*The dog is invited back into the vicinity.*

*He is given social attention.*

approaching the dog and waiting until the he yields and shows submissive behaviour towards the owner. The dog has to distance himself and, as a result, loses direct proximity to the person, which constitutes a negative punishment.

If he accepts this constraint and communicates with his owner instead of with the other dog, he should be left standing for a short time to process what he has learned and to avoid switching too quickly between punishment and reinforcement. Only then is he called back to his owner with an inviting gesture. This invitation is negative reinforcement, because the unpleasant distance to the owner is removed.

Once he is back near his owner again, the dog has another chance to behave differently. If he is friendly, his behaviour is rewarded with social attention, physical contact, quiet stroking or even food. This part is positive reinforcement.

The benefits are that the dog has to leave and the owner does not run away. The owner is also in charge in the conflict and therefore shows confident conflict behaviour. Furthermore, it is immediately possible for your dog to approach the other dog again and the technique can be repeated until the dog changes his behaviour and cooperates with the owner.

The disadvantage is that the technique is based on body language and physical tension alone and people nowadays have difficulty expressing themselves with their body and controlling it. Learning to dance can help you to develop a great feel for your own body at the same time.

If the approach is successful, the next step could even involve the owner acting as a social learning role model for their dog. With your dog on his lead, walk straight up to another dog and try to make friendly contact with it. If your own dog behaves aggressively, send him away as described and leave him to stand a short distance away. Then turn to the other dog and pet it. If this causes your own dog to attack, make him distance himself from you once again. If he accepts your decision to pat the other dog and remains in his designated position, invite to come forward (to his owner and therefore also to the other dog). If he behaves aggressively again when he arrives, send him away. If he is still being friendly, allow him to stay, give him positive feedback and perhaps allow him to make contact with the other dog, if possible. Of course, at this stage of training the dog should already be able to be guided by people so that the owner can convey their mood to the dog.

# The end of learning theory is the beginning of the relationship

So that's cleared everything up. The most effective thing is actually to punish unwanted behaviour on the lead and to reward the desired behaviour. All too often in this area of dog training, we come across a kind of "either/or" question of belief. I either assert myself against my dog or I am nice and reward him. The emotional division of people into good and evil according to how they use learning theory creates polar opposites and the positions of the opposing parties become entrenched. Reinforcement and punishment are neither character traits nor are they mutually exclusive, so why not use both if it makes sense? – perhaps because this combination of learning theories is professionally and emotionally the most difficult?

You should ask yourself the following question first: am I currently able to teach my dog alternative behaviour, to reliably interrupt his unwanted behaviour for a certain period at the appropriate intensity and correct timing, without anger but with goodwill and conviction and, in turn, to then help him to feel that he can safely find an alternative with me and perceive it to be pleasant, but without encouraging him to be aggressive again?

I think that few of you could answer this question with "yes", because if you could do that now, you probably wouldn't be reading this book. However, this means that the basic requirements for working directly on the conflict are missing, which is strange, seeing as learning theory is so simple.

## Fortunately, human-dog relationships are more than just learning theory

People don't just get dogs for no reason; dogs have a function for their owners. We place expectations on them and subject them to our training patterns and strategies. In order to work on a problem seriously, it is important to see yourself as part of the problem, but also as part of the solution. We now need to take a closer look at our relationship and conflict behaviour so far and make it transparent. Only when you have established your position and reflected upon it will you know what changes you need to make to be able to achieve your goals. That doesn't just sound like work; it is. But your dog is supposed to change too, after all. Our deep respect for punitive measures is good for our dogs and for us too, because banging your fist on the table might give you some breathing space, but it doesn't change anything. Many things have to be examined and trained first, before you can eventually say "Leave it be; do something else for a change." But who is talking to whom here?

# Relationship
## and diagnosis

Every consultation must be preceded by a diagnosis. The diagnostic picture of the owner-dog relationship is the first and most important step in the consultation. If, as a dog trainer, I am equipped with plenty of specialist knowledge about dogs and activities that I can do with them, I do not need to worry about the subsequent practical training, but training ideas and techniques are of little use if I haven't understood the relationship. It would be short-sighted to simply assess the dog's behaviour against a background of specialist knowledge.

## Diagnostics and self-clarification

Making the diagnosis helps both me, as a trainer, and the client. As a consultant, I first have to try to understand the relationship between the owner and the dog. Only then can I analyse the problem, explain it with theories and work out a sensible solution

If I don't grasp the relationship, I can only give generalised tips that usually do not lead to any lasting improvement. Diagnosis is important for clients because it helps them with self-clarification. People are a part of the system, so they often do not recognise their own structures and processes in the relationship and, consequently, cannot understand them. However, if I know where I stand, I can also decide on my final destination, examine it more closely and plan how to get there. That is what the initial consultation is for. Don't be confused by the name, because an initial consultation may take place in one meeting,

*The initial consultation is not an examination, but a discussion with the aim of self-clarification for the owner.*

but it may also be extended over several meetings or it may be necessary between practical sessions.

*Dogs have sneaked their way into our homes and then into our hearts,
so looking at the owner–dog relationship is something very intimate.
(Photo: Nadin Matthews)*

## Training consultation may have a profound effect

Diagnosis means perceiving/seeing something clearly. It takes a while, perhaps even the entire duration of the consultation, until this is possible. Diagnosis means becoming aware, perceiving, understanding, analysing and explaining reasons for acting, thinking and feeling that have previously been subconscious and in the background. When this happens, previous disruptive behaviour can become receptive to another decision. It can be unlearned, integrated or changed. The solution to the problem does not necessarily entail the dog no longer showing the behaviour. Perhaps the owner will just find another way of dealing with it. Dog owners usually cannot set this process in motion alone, because individual and systemic defence mechanisms and resistance prevent this kind of development of awareness. Relationships and training can be very intimate areas because both training and relationship behaviour are based on our own experiences. These behaviours have usually been learned a long time ago and encompass the major themes in life such as reliability, closeness, distance, disappointment, fear, loss, love, trust, security and protection. This area is usually well protected in people and the protection provided by defence can prevent insights from being made, and it is often difficult to break through it alone. Diagnosis therefore does not just mean identifying the fundamental problem correctly, but is primarily based on understanding people and the behavioural ideas that they have developed. Can that be the role of a dog trainer? Perhaps the dog trainer's role should move away from dog training and towards training consultation.

## Communication analysis

In order to introduce change, it is important to expose the "old" structures first. What emotional function does the dog perform for its owner? What expectations does the owner have for his dog? What expectations does the dog have for his owner? How do functions and expectations influence communication and therefore also the roles? What training ideas and skills does the owner have? What strategies do the owner and dog follow in a conflict?

The questions show that it is not just about the dog and not just about the owner, but what comes in between. In everyday communication, owner and dog define their self-image, their image of each other and that of their relationship. From this, structures and roles arise that enable them to predict each other's behaviour. This is a major advantage because it makes coexistence predictable. However, when difficulties arise in the relationship, both sides will show conflict behaviour that corresponds to their role. That can be a disadvantage and may sometimes even prevent a conflict from being resolved.

## Roles or gridlock

In social groups, fixed rules and patterns for mutual communication become established in relationships. Fixed roles develop when interaction patterns become rehearsed and predictable, so we may keep observing the same interaction patterns in humans and dogs in certain situations. As a result, each behaviour pattern can be predicted and each party expects that the other will continue to behave in this way. For example, the owner assumes that the dog will behave aggressively and the dog assumes that the owner will try to stop him.

However, roles are context-specific and may change according to the situation. Owners and dogs may assume several roles within a relationship, for example, a dog can be a little ray of sunshine in domestic coexistence and a troublemaker outdoors or the comfort-blanket in the house and the boss outside. Each role has its function within the system. Here is an overview of some typical roles: the "ray of sunshine" is friendly and creates a good atmosphere; the "example" is capable and makes his owners proud; the "clown" is funny, cheering and takes his owners' mind off unpleasant thoughts and feelings; the "one-man

*The "worrier" takes attention away from other problems.*
*(Photo: Nadin Matthews)*

dog" is responsible and helps his owner, for example, with training their second (usually problematic) dog; the "worrier" is weighed down by problems or illness and takes attention away from other issues, uniting his owners in concern; the "troublemaker" is annoying, but also takes attention away from other issues and unites the owners in discipline; the "black sheep" acts out his owner's taboo wishes (such as expressing feelings without embarrassment), takes on all of the negative projections and unites his owners in setting boundaries.

The roles make sense, even though they seem very negative at first. The disadvantage of roles is that somebody is not "allowed" to show any other behaviour patterns within their role or rather, these other behaviour patterns are not even perceived when they are shown, so they are shown even less frequently as a result. The role-specific interaction patterns are perpetuated by the meaning that underlies them, the expectations of both parties and the corresponding role of the owner. In order to introduce change, roles initially have to be clarified in order to weaken or break them down. On the one hand, change consists of the owner assigning him- or herself a new role and fulfilling it and, on the other hand, allowing the dog to leave his old role and helping him into the new role.

A dog's status rises if he takes on many of the important roles in his owner's life, for example, if he is the comfort-blanket on lonely evenings, the clown during the day who makes his owner laugh and forget about their everyday worries and the exemplary dog at family gatherings who fills his owner with pride and helps them to feel better about themselves. The dog doesn't just feel important; he is important. It is not really surprising then that this dog also takes control in conflict situations. Dogs are practically forced into some roles, for example, the conflict approaches, the owner looks questioningly at his dog and lets him make the decision. To bring about change, it makes sense to scrutinise the other roles in daily coexistence to see if they are fuelling the problem. And that brings us to a topic that goes far beyond dog training. We call it consultation.

## "Who are you, then?" Learning and relationships

There are a number of dog trainers in Germany and each one claims to understand about dog behaviour, but you don't find the real experts at dog training clubs. Instead, you find them in places where people walk their dogs. To begin with, they seem inconspicuous, randomly standing at the edge of the park, where they pretend to be letting their own dog play. But, believe me, that's just a disguise. They wait until you are feeling confident with your problem dog, innocuously strike up a conversation, turn the subject around to your dog and snap! The trap shuts: you are being forcibly advised! You get a concise analysis of your dog's behaviour, origins, thoughts and feelings and, after around five minutes, there it is: the tip, the one, crucial tip for you and your dog. This degree of precision still impresses me today and it is something I can't do. Perhaps it is precisely this inability that fills the pages of this book. Imagine opening a dog book and all it says inside is "You just have to be really assertive and throw him on his back!" This is followed by pages of bibliographical references and then it ends. Or imagine a book that says "You need lots of love and patience and you must reward your dog with food whenever he does something right." This long sentence will also be followed by an index.

Well, if only life were that simple. I don't believe that problems can be solved just by applying learning theory. Either I am making things complicated or I am right and it is actually not that easy, but it could also be a bit of both.

Take ten people with lead-aggressive dogs and instruct them to reward their dogs with food for showing the right behaviour and to interrupt the incorrect behaviour with an action. The results you achieve will differ. This is obviously partly because of the different dogs, their level of motivation and their interest in food, but it is also because of their owners' respective ability to exert a social influence. Or to put it another way, dogs' learning behaviour depends on who is doing the rewarding or punishing, among other

*How would the dog
describe his owner?*

things. Are you equally happy about praise, no matter who gives it? Do you accept every prohibition, no matter who it comes from? – probably not.

How people and dogs assess themselves, their social counterparts and their relationship together is crucial. Reinforcement and punishment are a kind of social feedback and evaluation of the behaviour in question. When we reward or punish, we are expressing what we thought about our dog's previous action. But how much does he care about what we think? So far we have been looking into the question of what significance your dog has for you, but now it is time to consider: who am I for my dog?

As I see it, the following four factors favour the acceptance of reward and punishment and so determine the required intensity: popularity, high status, social skills and expertise!

## Popularity

If you like somebody their opinion is important to you. You try to get as close to and as much recognition from this social partner as possible. You associate this person with happy times. He or she can be a dog owner who brings excitement and fun into the relationship, relaxes the group with their exuberance and good mood or livens it up with adventure and action. This could include wild games, as well as leaving the normal paths on a walk and always finding new ideas for shared activities. However, a person who thoughtfully cares for their dog, perceives his needs and meets them, relaxes the group with quietness and cuddles and can be relied upon to provide food can be attractive for a dog and therefore very popular.

## Status and the capacity to assert oneself

People who make decisions guided from within and who do not have any problems with self-presentation and feel confident when interacting with others can lead a group well. There is an art to communicating your own needs and boundaries clearly and putting these requirements into practice. People like this can be very impressive and their feedback is important for others. Their own confidence and clear actions also give a dog confidence. What somebody like this says carries weight, it is unambiguous and readily accepted by dogs.

## Social skills

People who are competent in social situations are often asked for advice. The opinion of somebody like this is important to people because they feel that they are being taken seriously and given good advice. People with good social skills are able to express themselves appropriately without suppressing the concerns of others. That includes accepting the dog as an individual personality, the ability to empathise with him and to reflect upon their own training behaviour. People with good social skills understand the dog but also appreciate the needs of others. For dogs, they represent a friendly basis in the shared relationship.

## Expertise

Imagine you are planning and building yourself a house. Your neighbours, who built themselves a terrible house and a reputable architect compliment you on your achievement. Whose opinion is more important to you? Specialist knowledge doesn't just impress people. In the owner-dog relationship, expertise can reduce misunderstandings in communication. For example, if a person can explain why a dog behaves in a certain way, they will not be disappointed or angry at the wrong time.

If somebody understands a lot about something, they will be taken seriously. Dogs can solve tasks more quickly if they have been devised using specialist knowledge. The dog will also register that this person is easy to understand. For dogs, professional skills are expressed by clearly formulated goals, the right timing and a sense of proportion, among other things.

# Aptitude and understanding roles

Each of the human skills described influences the relationship and learning behaviour of the dog. Successful training involves bringing all of these skills together.

However, people have many different skills and are not gifted in all areas. They cultivate their role as trainer according to their respective talents and look for training approaches that correspond to them. You can choose anything, from uncompromising subordination to constant occupation and from "no food without achievement" to professionally well-founded conflict avoidance.

It isn't a problem when everything is going well, but when difficulties arise with the dog, being very gifted in just one of these areas can be a disadvantage. Each of these roles has a downside if it is taken too far. In the following, I will try to show the extremes of the following roles and the skills associated with them. The result is highly differentiated archetypes that maybe do not exist in this extreme form in reality. Fortunately, real life is a little more colourful. However, exaggeration can help you to discover your own behavioural tendencies and to see where gaining more skills would be useful.

## "Somebody who is only ever funny…"
The eternal joker – very popular

Jokers are very popular because they make other people laugh and draw attention to themselves with constant new ideas. However, they tend to not take conflicts seriously and to gloss over things, in the truest sense of the word. They are not asked for advice about serious issues because they stop where the fun stops. They lack social skills and expertise, as well as the ability to assert themselves.

## "Somebody who is only ever nice…"
The eternal carer – very popular

Eternal carers are a blessing for everyone. They help others and lend a shoulder to cry on when something goes wrong. But people stop listening to the carer when questions about decisions come up. The eternal carer tends to harmonise and avoid conflicts. If

*Fun, games and exuberance are important for dogs.*
*But are they enough to train a dog?*

*Even if people would like it, not every problem*
*can be stroked away. (Photo: Nadin Matthews)*

*Just because the dog behaves doesn't mean the relationship is working. (Photo: Nadin Matthews)*

conflict is unavoidable, their strategy is to endure and sit tight, rather than intervene. They have not developed their own standing because they are always supporting others and can be overlooked in conflicts as a result. If somebody only makes the sandwiches, then that is how they will be seen.

## "Somebody who is only ever assertive..."

### The eternal enforcer – high status

Eternal enforcers strive like no others for power and to enforce their own will. They are mainly around when it comes to making decisions. People do what the enforcer says because they do not want any trouble and because they know that the enforcer has the upper hand. Therefore, enforcers are very well suited to wrapping up conflicts and asserting themselves against others. However, they do not have to be competent or popular to maintain their position. Others do not enjoy making friends with them and only do so because they are under pressure. As a result, the enforcer always stands with his or her back against the wall, always having to control the others and never able to relax. The enforcer is not somebody you would ever ask for advice, but somebody that you listen to. There is a difference! Trust and emotional bonds fall by the wayside.

## "Somebody who wants to do everything right..."

### The eternal advisor – social skills

Eternal advisors help others to make decisions. They give information about various possible

*The socially skilled advisor helps with decisions, without insisting on the outcome.*

courses of action and, as a result, influence the decision, but in the end do not make the decision themselves. Their advice ends before the decision and begins again afterwards. In conflicts, they tend to explain the behaviour of everybody involved and mediate between the parties, rather than actually acting on their own account as a knowledgeable person. Advisors are advisors and not the head of the company.

## "Somebody who is always well informed…"

### The eternal specialist – expertise

Nobody knows more about a topic than the specialists. They are extremely well-read, intelligent and can, for example, list and plan learning processes in detail. When it comes to conflicts, experts tend to acquire more

*The dog acts while the specialist ponders and weighs up the pros and cons.*

*There are no universal laws that apply to harmonious interaction between owner and dog. (Photo: Nadin Matthews)*

specialist knowledge in the hope it will help them to find a solution. The expert tries to explain problems in a purely professional way, whereas decisions on social matters are usually made on an emotional level. While the specialist is still thinking and pondering, others acted with their gut instinct long ago and brought about the decision. Social relationships cannot be made technical.

## The more important you are, the less you have to do

Who are you for your dog? Who would you like to be? What roles would you have to take on so that your dog could give up his? We all have strengths and weaknesses, convictions and insecurities. Taking a look at yourself and what you bring to the relationship with your dog in terms of skills can help you to see what you still need to learn. If the dog is to change, we need to change ourselves first. Sometimes you just need to remember your own skills, but at other times it may be necessary to expand them. Dogs tell us about shortcomings in training, they reflect our skills as well as our secret wishes and can help us to develop further in our own personalities, based on the problem in question. We should be thankful for every problem, because problems give us the opportunity to learn something new. People who represent more for their dog have to do less for their dog to enjoy rewards or accept boundaries.

The dream of a popular owner, who is characterised by calmness, fairness, social skills and expertise, as well as decisiveness, might not always come true, but troubled times necessitate change. Not just change in the dog but in the person who has taken on the task of training. If we only use our strengths and only try training approaches that correspond to our talents, the dog and his own needs may be overlooked and that would not be fair. Training should focus on the recipient, not on the trainer.

## Problem analysis

Problem analysis involves linking up all of the aspects of relationship, training and conflict behaviour, taking into consideration the individual personalities and against the background of specialist knowledge about canine development, factors for aggressive behaviour, genetics, learning behaviour and body language, and analysing them in relation to the problem. This gives a description of the ACTUAL situation in the owner-dog relationship. Using this approach, we come across many different people, dogs and relationships and each of these relationships is unique.

There is a whole host of questions to be asked in order to become more familiar with the problem. How does the problem situation usually play out? Who does what? Who feels what? What effects does the problem have on your relationship with your dog? How do the people in your environment react to it? When did the problem arise for the first time? How did you react to it? Has the problem changed over the course of time? How did you notice? What would have to happen to make the problem worse? How would you know if the problem were no longer there? What would change as a result? What problem were you dealing with before the current problem arose? Which problems would you have, if you didn't have this problem? What would the solution have to look like, what would it have to involve for you to be able to accept it? What kind of solution could you not imagine at all? How have you managed other conflicts in the past?

A problem is the expression of a disruption in the system as a whole. Therefore, analysis is not just about describing the problem, but the behavioural connections. What does the role of the dog in the house have to do with his behaviour on the walk? What does defensive aggression have to do with the dog's origins? What does the owner's need for closeness have to do with the dog's aggressive behaviour? What does the dog's appetitive behaviour at the beginning of the walk have to do with how well the dog is kept occupied? What does the dog's unwillingness to connect with his owner have to do with the owner's very assertive behaviour?

It is not about simple causal effects, but an initial, preliminary interpretation of behaviour. When examining the system, the dog is to be regarded as a fully paid-up member of the pack that is every bit as involved in communication as his owner. The diagnosis should be free from finger-pointing and characterised by the trainers' empathy. Empathy is not a technique! Consultation is not about selling your methods or subjugating dog owners to your own attitude.

**1**

*When dogs meet, they confront each other with their personal self-image. Some are big; others feel big.*

**2**

*Some people worry about holding onto their dog and about being pulled over. Others worry about their dog and are afraid he will be bitten.*

**3**

*Aggressive behaviour looks similar in little and large, but the stories behind it are not visible to the naked eye.*

**4**

*In the end, everybody goes back to the place where self-image is recreated every-day: home.*

# The change
## and the
# challenge

If a person is suffering because of a conflict, this conflict turns into a problem. A problem can be identified as something you muse over and reformulate a great deal, but for which you do not have a solution. A problem usually involves hopelessness. If you were being positive you could also see a problem as a riddle, i.e. there is a solution – you just haven't found it yet. To find the solution, you need to think about the riddle, instead of pushing it to the back of your mind. That also includes changing the way you look at the problem, from hopeless to constructive, for example, because of the new positive angle. From "Why does it have to happen to me?" to "What can I do to make myself feel better?" Changes are not techniques but begin in your head and in your heart. If they feel strange and unfamiliar, it's because they are.

## Objectives

Formulating goals is an important step in the initial consultation. This is how most dog owners define their goal: "I want him to stop doing it!" This goal is very difficult because only the dog is supposed to change and the owner does not even come into the

*Owners can learn about setting clear goals from their dog. (Photo: Nadin Matthews)*

equation. It is very similar to lead aggression, where the dog "does" and the owner disappears into the background. How about the following goal? "I would like to have a greater influence over my dog's behaviour when we meet other dogs" or "I would like to invite my dog to work with me, even when another dog is approaching." We are almost at the end of the book and it is time to abandon the hope of a spontaneous improvement. Believe me, it won't get better as he gets older. But behaviour can change. Become an active participant in your relationship with your dog. In any case, hope is a lonely feeling if it always dies in the end. In exactly the same way as people, dogs need a reason to change. Who should give the dog this reason? Please don't ask your neighbour this time.

## Relationship change

Dogs know their owners inside and out, the respective roles have been established and work on the problem itself is very rarely possible. If you want to be heard in a conflict, you should already have communicated convincingly within the relationship that you can manage this too. However, in most cases, something quite different has been communicated up until this point and this is something that dogs do not forget from one day to the next. Therefore, redefinition of roles is usually the first step towards change. After all, subsequent training should fall on fertile soil.

Nowhere is communication more intimate, uninhibited and authentic than in everyday domestic life. Home is the place where most people do not experience any problems

and are relaxed. It provides a good place, a good atmosphere and a secure framework for the initial changes. These changes can follow different goals.

Sometimes the first changes are initially only there to prevent the worst by safeguarding and avoiding conflict; sometimes the self-resolving component makes them the solution to the problem; sometimes they change the roles and status of the owner and dog; sometimes they help the owner to reflect upon or regain his own training behaviour; sometimes they upset the apple cart in order to weaken old structures and create space for new ones; sometimes they train owners and dogs in establishing new learning experiences; sometimes they sow the seeds for subsequent practical work with the owner-dog team; and sometimes they act as a kind of reset button to make a new start possible.

Change makes change. But which direction should you take? What foundations do dog and owner need? Each change in the relationship should be individual and adapted to the owner and the dog as well as to the problem and the respective relationship status. Unfortunately, I don't know anything about you and your dog, so I can only argue using examples and create an overview of the possibilities. After working out the relationship and problem structure, I like to give the first changes a kind of heading, a motto and a unique goal that represents a first interim objective on the way to the solution, but that goes hand-in-hand with the overall aim of the consultation.

Imagine a dog that barks in frustration at other dogs when he is on his lead. His owners describe him as frantic, uninhibited, loud, demanding, but also as a clown who makes

*When one person in the relationship changes, the others change with them, even if they are sceptical at first.*
*(Photo: Nadin Matthews)*

them laugh. They are actually rather quiet but have already adapted to their dog's frantic nature and feel stressed. They are very considerate and try to do everything right for the dog, meeting his needs in the hope that he would then be satisfied and give them some peace. They don't enjoy going places with their dog, because it is so stressful and they prefer to do without trips because they feel guilty about not taking him with them. They get fewer and fewer visitors because their dog annoys the guests. This description is admittedly inadequate, but I hope that it is enough to give you an example. The motto for changes in the home could be: "Calmness leads to success; commotion leads to failure."

For the owners, this means starting to make their own decisions again, making space for calmness and their own life, taking this calmness as the default mood for situations and making it possible for the dog to perceive calmness as the successful strategy and commotion as the unsuccessful strategy. If you adopt the motto into your system as a new rule and apply it to every difficult situation, your life will change dramatically. You do not need to make a lot of changes, just appropriate changes that are then reflected in all of your reaction patterns.

Below, I have listed a few key points to give a practical explanation of possible relationship changes. According to the diagnosis in

*Changes start inside and cannot
be imposed from the outside.*

each individual case, some of these points may be relevant for change and others not. Their intensity and orientation must be adapted in each case.

## Adjusting and re-evaluating your own role

The most important point is to think about role allocations. What roles have I given my dog and how can I release him from them or change them? Does he have to be the clown or am I unable to cheer myself up? Does he have to be the black sheep or am I incapable of expressing my feelings towards others? Does he have to be the worrier or am I not able to take care of myself or the issues in my life? Does he have to be the eternal child or can I let him grow up too? It is also important to examine your own behaviour patterns. Why do I need so much control? What would happen if I let go of the reins? Why do I need so much harmony? What would happen if I set boundaries? It is perhaps sometimes a case of exposing the dog as a dog, giving him more credit for being a dog and asking yourself whether, as a human, you can be disappointed by a dog.

What is the point of this? It helps to allow a change to become authentic. The owner's new attitude and prevailing mood is expressed through their body language. For example, if somebody ignores their dog because the dog trainer has told them that they should, they will ignore the dog as if they have been told to do so by somebody else and not because their attitude towards the dog has changed. They will maybe look intently to the side when the dog approaches; turn away when he puts

them under pressure; and eventually leave the room because they can't stand it any longer. Anybody that has even the slightest interest in body language will quickly notice that this kind of behaviour is anything but successful self-presentation. But if somebody wants to get their life back after all the adaptations and introduces the changes according to the maxim "I don't have to do anything, but I know who I am and what I want", then that is how they will walk around – with a proudly puffed-up chest, behaving in their own way, confident and accountable to none. With this basic attitude, you don't have to ignore the dog: you can look at him and even speak to and pat him. The inner impression makes the expression.

## Safeguarding/avoidance

To avoid the dangers that some dogs pose, it is very sensible to make difficult moments safer to begin with. If you can assume that your dog will turn on you aggressively during meetings with other dogs, it makes sense to move your walks to dog-free areas during the initial phase. Safeguards in the form of a muzzle or canine headcollar are also possible. If the owner no longer has any form of control over the dog, he could think about avoiding walks completely during the first week. However, this should only be done in emergencies and if the dog has access to a garden.

## Instinct-guided behaviour/making decisions

If an owner is not taken seriously by his dog because his only talent is being caring, it can

*If dogs become a danger to people, safeguarding is indispensible during the process of change. (Photo: Nadin Matthews)*

help if the owner concentrates on himself and his own needs first. Did I really want to do that or have I allowed myself to be manipulated? Conscious awareness of your own wishes and interests is an important step for this.

## Unsettling

If systems are very gridlocked or if the owner is even being threatened by his dog, temporary unpredictability can provide the necessary unsettlement for new structures to be accepted. The owner's behaviour becomes more haphazard and unsettles the dog. Typical rituals take a different course to normal. The owner behaves in a way that the dog finds surprising and that is inconsistent with his expectations. As a result, the dog becomes more attentive, but also more insecure. This temporarily improves the status of the owner and makes the dog wish for the return of predictable patterns, which must then follow. For the predictable patterns to return, the owner's personality must "grow again", because if the dog is constantly questioning his owner, the owner has to have the right answers. Otherwise, the situation will lead to both owner and dog becoming insecure.

## Reassurance/social reliability

If a dog is rather insecure and his owner has confused him by coming up with more and more new training methods and ways of behaving, a clear structure can help. On the one hand, this applies to the daily routine and, on the other hand, to the owner's behaviour. The change makes life easier for the dog to understand and, at the same time, creates security for him. "When one thing happens, another thing will happen afterwards." Part of this involves working on getting used to worrying situations. The reliable structure enables dogs to embark on new things more easily. The owner must also be a self-confident presence in conflict situations that come from the outside, by going first, supporting his dog socially and offering him protection. "I'm here now and you're not alone anymore."

## Demand more space for yourself

"I'm giving everything and getting nothing in return." When everything is about the dog and the problem, it can make it easier for the

*Dogs need enough space for themselves and their interests. (Photo: Nadin Matthews)*

owner and the dog if the owner devotes himself to his own things and becomes an active participant again. That can mean getting lots of space in the literal sense, finding a new hobby or rekindling interpersonal relationships and not allowing the dog to be involved in everything. A dog can only take guidance from somebody if this person sets the tone.

## Giving more space

"Giving more space" is the counterpart of "demanding more space" and means giving dogs that are socially overloaded or stressed enough space for themselves. Times when they do not have to meet any demands, including emotional demands like being stroked. In "wild" households there is a "quiet area" that is not in the middle of everyday goings-on. The opportunity to run free, i.e. without a lead, can be included in these measures.

## Closeness

Closeness is an interesting topic and, like everything else in life, it has two sides. For example, closeness can mean giving a dog a lot of attention to intentionally boost his self-confidence. Over-trained dogs, in particular, who have little self-confidence and who are insecure, can be made more confident with this social feedback. Closeness can also be used in different ways, for example, to knock an ignorant dog that likes to withdraw in the house out of its stride. You could put the dog on his lead and then attach the lead to your belt and move around the house as if everything were normal. The dog has to go with the person everywhere and maintain the contact.

## Tolerance of frustration

Dogs that find it difficult to cope with limitations in having their needs satisfied should be confronted with such limitations during the initial phase of the change. Adequate tolerance of frustration is an important prerequisite for subsequent tolerance of provocation by other dogs. Here, the training keywords are "postponement of praise".

Put the dog in a situation where he expects his needs to be satisfied and only fulfil these needs when his expectant behaviour diminishes and he calms down. For example, make his food, but don't give it to him and do something else instead. If, after a while, the dog stops expressing his frustration, accepts the situation and retreats, give him the food.

You can try something similar when you let him off his lead at the park. Stand with your dog, who is brimming over with excitement, in the park where all of the other dogs are already playing, but do not let him off his lead. When he calms down, he can run with the others. If he doesn't calm down, he will have to go home again without playing off his lead. The exercises you develop must involve an element of frustration, but they must also be appropriate and involve a pleasant solution for the dog. The dog is supposed to learn to be able to tolerate frustration, not to learn how to be more frustrated.

## Husbandry

Nowadays, it is less common and the relevant target group would hardly be reading a book like this, but, nevertheless, dogs need adequate time off their lead! The expectation

*Adequate frustration tolerance is a basic requirement for handling provocation from other dogs. (Photo: Nadin Matthews)*

that a dog should walk quietly on his lead is not appropriate if the dog is only walked around the block for fifteen minutes, three times a day. The same applies to relationships where the dog is alone all day, only gets out on his lead in the evening and then behaves aggressively. As distance runners, dogs justifiably become frustrated. Changing the prevailing conditions (for example, by employing a dog walker) makes more sense than training the dog.

## Activities

In relationships where there is little common ground between the owner and dog, it can be beneficial to look for a shared "hobby" where you can experience something positive

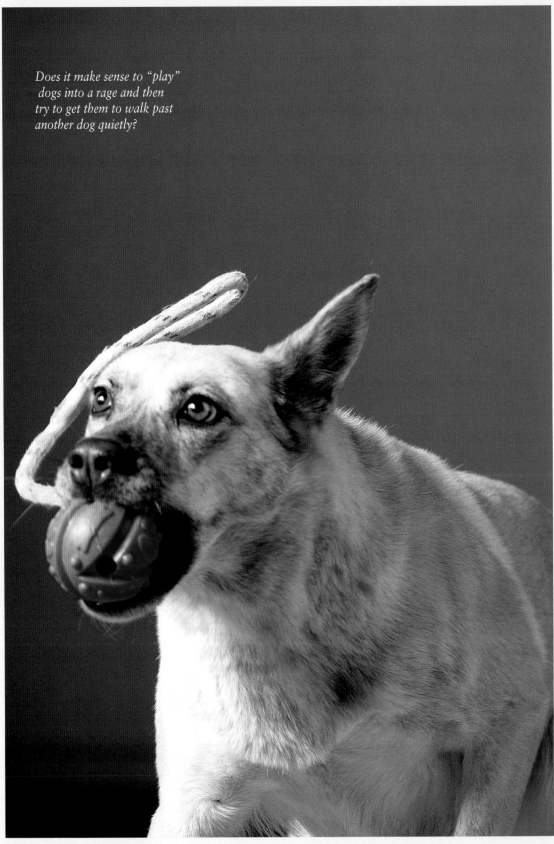

*Does it make sense to "play" dogs into a rage and then try to get them to walk past another dog quietly?*

together again. In relationships that are characterised by non-stop fun, a temporary phasing down of activities can create relaxation and clarity and sometimes only this may allow serious work on the problem.

## Reducing the dog's standard of living/withdrawal of important resources

If the dog is oversaturated socially or materially, lowering his standard of living can make him more accessible again. For example, this could entail reduction of leisure activities, expressions of affection, spatial restrictions or not meeting demands.

## New consequences for old behaviour

Because the solution to the conflict does not come at the beginning of the work, dog owners initially need temporary strategies in order to deal with anticipated conflict. If

*Change doesn't just feel strange to owners.*

possible, the "old" problem behaviour should lead to new consequences or different reactions from the owner. This does not get rid of the problem, but it won't make it worse.

For dogs that are aggressive for social reasons and are not insecure, you could try the following. The owner suddenly stops evaluating barking on the lead with his body language, voice and gaze. If possible, barking could instead lead to the dog being tied to a tree and the owner continuing alone or even going over to the other dog and striking up a conversation with its owner.

For dogs that are frantic, demanding and take themselves very seriously, the walk could even begin differently. If the dog gets overexcited at the door when the owner announces that they want to go for a walk, this could result in the dog first having his lead put on and then being brushed or taken into a room that has no attraction for him. The owner could also leave the house alone with the lead in his hand, pretending to have forgotten the dog, but of course return after a short time to collect him.

## Rewarding desired behaviour

Since the problem behaviour is no longer being evaluated by the owner, the dog has the opportunity to show different behaviour. If this behaviour is desired or an approximation of the desired behaviour, it makes sense to reward it, sometimes just with attention and closeness and sometimes with food or improving the situation (for example, taking the dog off its lead, and so on). In particular, behaviour patterns that aid cooperation should be seen and reinforced.

## Making things unpleasant for the dog

Dogs do not always accept changes in their owners immediately and can write lengthy letters of complaint in the form of unwanted behaviours. For example, if the dog barks at his owner because the owner is devoting himself to his own concerns and not being controlled by the dog, the answer should entail deterioration of the dog's situation and not harm the owner's self-presentation. It makes sense to take the dog by the collar without say-

1
*It is easier to connect to somebody who pre-determines behaviour.*

ing anything and remove him from the room instead of rebuking him in the normal verbal manner. His demand for closeness and attention therefore has the opposite effect, namely, distance, and he can learn something from that.

# Transferring the new skills onto the lead

When the situation has become clearer for the owner and the dog and the changes feel almost normal, the next focus is mutual communication on the lead. The dog now gets the chance to learn to be guided by his owner when on the lead, without distraction, and to develop an alternative to aggressive behaviour. The owner has the chance to experience how it feels to cooperate with the dog, lead the conversation and take responsibility. The distraction can be intensified when both know what they are doing. What doesn't work without distractions definitely won't work with them. There are many techniques for walking a dog on a lead. When

|2

*A dog can relax when the owner confidently begins to take control and responsibility.*

|3

*On the one hand, this is an important basis for changing lead aggression and, on the other hand, it strengthens the emotional bond.*

*Proxy conflicts help people to practise*
*for real life in a safe environment.*
*(Photo: Nadin Matthews)*

choosing one, the aim of the consultation as a whole should be taken into consideration. If, for example, the owner used to be helpless in the conflict and would like to have more influence, it makes sense to experience these changes on a domestic level first, but also to continue them when walking on the lead. A new way of communicating on the lead is the basic requirement for changing lead aggression.

## Proxy conflicts

Along with the choice of learning technique, the way in which the owner puts the technique into practice is relevant for changing the problem in the long term. Negative feelings are often associated with previous encounters with dogs. If a person becomes stressed, they will tend to return to their old behaviour patterns, in a similar way to dogs. To train new conflict behaviour, including the new mood, it makes sense to try out new, inconsequential conflicts with the dog to begin with. Before working on lead aggression, you could try, for example, walking past a sausage or a flying ball. The dog will want to approach these things out of interest and, no matter what learning method you have chosen, you can try it out in a situation where there is a distraction, in a relaxed way. Only when the owner feels confident in putting the technique into practice and the dog can accept the owner's new behaviour can it be transferred onto real conflicts. Both will then have the opportunity to fall back on what they have learned. The owner knows they can do it and the dog does too. This also gives you the opportunity to test whether the dog has learnt enough or whether the chosen technique actually even works for the dog.

## Solving the riddle in real life

You have cleared up your relationship with your dog, given him a reason to look to you for guidance when he is on the lead, practised one or more methods for dealing with conflict, and now you want to try out your new skills in an encounter with another dog. Don't take on too much to begin with by training with public enemy no. 1 straightaway. Perhaps your dog will return to old patterns in an old conflict. Perhaps you will return to old actions because of old feelings. All of this is normal. A return does not mean a step back. Do not put yourself under pressure. You can give yourself more confidence by setting the prevailing conditions. For example, ask your neighbours whether they would be available to do a few exercises with your dog, practise in a strange city where you don't know anybody and a yapping dog will be less embarrassing, or get a dog trainer or best friend to accompany you in these first situations. Intentionally seek out conflicts and then you will be prepared for them. Real life will come along anyway, usually emerging from its driveway at around half past eight in the morning.

# Conclusion